GREAT SOURCE

Test Achiever

Mastering Standardized Tests

Grade 6

Test preparation for reading,
language arts, and mathematics

GReaT SOuRCe
EDUCATION GROUP
A Houghton Mifflin Company

Design and production by Publicom, Inc., Acton, Massachusetts

Printed in the United States of America

International Standard Book Number: 0-669-46462-7

2 3 4 5 6 7 8 9 10 - HS - 03 02 01 00 99 98

URL address: http://www.greatsource.com/

Pretest

READING: Vocabulary

Directions: Find the word that means the same, or almost the same, as the underlined word.

1. <u>acquire</u> a jacket

Ⓐ get Ⓒ lose
Ⓑ clean Ⓓ repair

2. a <u>jubilant</u> crowd

Ⓐ large Ⓒ joyous
Ⓑ angry Ⓓ foreign

3. <u>rotate</u> the bowl

Ⓐ wash Ⓒ fill
Ⓑ turn Ⓓ carry

4. <u>dormant</u> volcano

Ⓐ powerful Ⓒ dangerous
Ⓑ inactive Ⓓ enormous

5. standing on the <u>brink</u>

Ⓐ lawn Ⓒ edge
Ⓑ pavement Ⓓ top

6. <u>prosper</u> in business

Ⓐ fail Ⓒ cheat
Ⓑ trade Ⓓ succeed

Directions: Find the word that means the OPPOSITE of the underlined word.

7. a <u>worthwhile</u> project

Ⓐ complicated Ⓒ important
Ⓑ useless Ⓓ secret

8. a <u>bashful</u> boy

Ⓐ shy Ⓒ bold
Ⓑ timid Ⓓ proud

Directions: Read the two sentences. Find the word that best fits the meaning of **both** sentences.

9. Put the _____ of water on the table.

The _____ hurled the ball.

Ⓐ glass Ⓒ pitcher
Ⓑ coach Ⓓ player

10. There was a _____ trace of ink on the fabric.

Some people _____ if they get too hot.

Ⓐ faint Ⓒ collapse
Ⓑ slight Ⓓ mere

11. Did you _____ your finger in the door?

Put some _____ on your toast.

Ⓐ honey Ⓒ close
Ⓑ slam Ⓓ jam

Go On

READING: Vocabulary (continued)

Directions: Read the sentences. Choose the word that best completes the meaning of each sentence.

George was clearing the dinner dishes from the table. First he __(12)__ the five dinner dishes. As he carried them toward the sink, he __(13)__ on a small rag rug. His feet flew up in the air, and the __(14)__ slipped out of his grasp. Poor George ended up on the floor, surrounded by slivers of shattered china.

12.
- Ⓐ washed
- Ⓑ selected
- Ⓒ stacked
- Ⓓ dried

13.
- Ⓐ sat
- Ⓑ stood
- Ⓒ stayed
- Ⓓ slipped

14.
- Ⓐ plates
- Ⓑ washcloth
- Ⓒ food
- Ⓓ handle

Directions: Choose the meaning of the underlined prefix or suffix.

15. <u>non</u>member   <u>non</u>residential
- Ⓐ not
- Ⓑ against
- Ⓒ before
- Ⓓ without

16. <u>bi</u>cycle   <u>bi</u>lateral
- Ⓐ not
- Ⓑ forward
- Ⓒ two
- Ⓓ before

17. owner<u>ship</u>   friend<u>ship</u>
- Ⓐ without
- Ⓑ in the direction of
- Ⓒ one who
- Ⓓ state or quality of

18. histor<u>ical</u>   polit<u>ical</u>
- Ⓐ through
- Ⓑ state or quality of
- Ⓒ relating to
- Ⓓ lacking

Directions: Read the sentence and the question. Find the word that best answers the question.

19. Sasha _____ the slice of pizza.

Which word suggests greed and haste?
- Ⓐ gobbled
- Ⓑ nibbled
- Ⓒ ate
- Ⓓ finished

20. The dog _____ at the stranger.

Which word suggests danger?
- Ⓐ jumped
- Ⓑ lunged
- Ⓒ leaped
- Ⓓ hopped

21. My mother _____ that I mow the lawn before I went out to play.

Which word suggests force?
- Ⓐ demanded
- Ⓑ asked
- Ⓒ requested
- Ⓓ wished

Stop

READING: Comprehension

Directions: Read each passage. Choose the best answer to each question.

Who is Jackie Joyner-Kersee?

Jackie Joyner-Kersee is one of the greatest female stars of track and field. She has won three Olympic gold medals, yet she suffers from a serious health condition. Joyner-Kersee has asthma. When she was young, many people warned her about all the things she couldn't do. Instead of giving up, Joyner-Kersee worked with her doctor to manage the disease.

Today, Jackie Joyner-Kersee spends part of her time touring the country and telling others about asthma. She is reaching out to the nearly five million American children who have the disease. She emphasizes that without proper treatment, asthma can be a dark cloud on the horizon. However, if kids listen to their doctors, they can look forward to a future full of excitement and activity.

---

22. Which statement is an opinion?

Ⓐ Jackie Joyner-Kersee is one of the greatest female stars of track and field.

Ⓑ She has won three Olympic gold medals.

Ⓒ Joyner-Kersee has asthma.

Ⓓ She is reaching out to the nearly five million American children who have asthma.

23. Which title best states the main idea of this passage?

Ⓐ "Asthma—A Serious Health Risk"

Ⓑ "Star of Track and Field"

Ⓒ "How to Manage Asthma in Children"

Ⓓ "Track Star with Asthma Reaches Out"

24. What does the author mean by the sentence, "Asthma can be a dark cloud on the horizon"?

Ⓐ Asthma can represent a serious problem in the future.

Ⓑ Asthma is generally more serious in bad weather.

Ⓒ An asthma attack feels like a thunderstorm.

Ⓓ People who have asthma tend to be sad and depressed.

25. According to this passage, what is the most important thing that kids with asthma need to do?

Ⓐ play sports

Ⓑ take it easy

Ⓒ listen to their doctors

Ⓓ reach out to others with the same disease

Go On

How did fairs come to be?

Fairs have been around for a long time. In Europe during the Middle Ages, people did most of their business at fairs. Merchants from many countries would gather to sell items such as fur, leather, and glass. One of the most important fairs of the Middle Ages was held in a French city called Troyes. The system of "troy weights" used by the merchants there gradually spread through much of Europe and is still used today to weigh gold, silver, and precious stones.

St. Bartholomew's Fair was held in London every year until the middle of the 1800s. This English fair was famous for the sale of horses and for the plays put on by groups of traveling actors.

For centuries, merchants met at a fair in Timbuktu in what is now the African nation of Mali. Merchants from the South would bring gold and ivory, while those from the North would bring salt. In India, there was a centuries-old fair in Pushkar where you could buy camels or enjoy watching the camel races.

Today there are still fairs at regular times and places each year. However, most people nowadays attend fairs for amusement rather than to engage in commerce. Instead of buying horses or gold, modern fairgoers go on wild rides, toss things at targets, and stuff themselves with rich foods and sweets.

26. The passage says that today people go to fairs for fun "rather than to engage in commerce." Commerce means —

Ⓐ amusement

Ⓑ politics

Ⓒ religion

Ⓓ business

27. A fair held in France during the Middle Ages led to the development of —

Ⓐ the metric system

Ⓑ gold mines

Ⓒ troy weights

Ⓓ camel races

28. What did the fair at Pushkar and the St. Bartholomew's Fair have in common?

Ⓐ traveling actors

Ⓑ the sale of animals

Ⓒ the sale of gold

Ⓓ the use of special weights

29. Which of these events at fairs began most recently?

Ⓐ People went on wild rides.

Ⓑ People traded furs.

Ⓒ People watched plays.

Ⓓ People bought camels.

Go On

Kim Willard's Puppy University

Nationally known dog trainer Kim Willard is proud to announce the grand opening of the Allston campus of her Puppy University. Trainers at Puppy University's other three campuses across the state have been turning out well-behaved graduates for over ten years. Using Kim's patented training techniques, Puppy University professors teach *all* dogs to behave better—whether they are family pets, working animals, or show dogs.

Untrained canines are a nuisance or, even worse, a danger. They irritate neighbors with their barking, destroy furniture, jump up on strangers, and run away from home. Some dogs even attack other animals or people.

At Puppy University, your dog will lose all these irritating behaviors. Using the same methods as Kim uses, trainers will teach you how to take command of your dog. Dogs are social animals that want to follow a leader; you just need to learn how to give the right commands. After graduation, your dog will follow your orders instantly, just like the prize-winning show dogs you see on Kim's weekly TV program, "Canine Champions."

---

30. What conclusion can you draw from this passage?

   Ⓐ Kim Willard is not a real dog trainer.

   Ⓑ Kim Willard does not actually teach at Puppy University.

   Ⓒ There are no other dog trainers in the state.

   Ⓓ All untrained dogs are dangerous.

31. Which statement supports the idea that untrained dogs are a nuisance?

   Ⓐ Dogs want to follow a leader.

   Ⓑ They just need the right commands.

   Ⓒ Dogs are social animals.

   Ⓓ They irritate neighbors with their barking.

32. According to the author, what makes dogs misbehave?

   Ⓐ strict owners

   Ⓑ other dogs

   Ⓒ a lack of leadership

   Ⓓ too much hard work

33. The writer tries to persuade people to bring their dogs to Puppy University mainly by suggesting that –

   Ⓐ their dogs will act like prize-winners

   Ⓑ there are three other campuses of Puppy University

   Ⓒ untrained dogs are dangerous

   Ⓓ Puppy University is for all dogs

Go On →

Tagging Along

The lawn was covered with tables of old china, worn-out shoes, and rusty, broken tools. Old-fashioned dresses and coats flapped from a clothesline, each with a price tag attached.

"Let's get out of here!" hissed Jess to her mother. "I've got a soccer game in less than half an hour." But Jess's mother didn't hear her. She had her head stuck halfway in an old trunk full of ancient hats and weird-looking purses. She pulled out a beaded evening bag and a feathered bonnet.

"These will be perfect for my antique store," she called to her daughter.

"Mom," sighed Jess in exasperation. "We left home an hour ago to get me some new soccer cleats before the game. So far we've been to four tag sales and you've bought eight pieces of old junk!"

"Correction," said her mother. "I've picked up eight valuable items for only a few dollars. Can't you wear your old cleats for just one more game?"

"That's what you said last week," scowled Jess, "when we stopped at the Ten-Family Tag Sale for 'just a minute' and ended up staying for two hours!"

"Sorry," smiled her mom, "but you have to admit it was worth it. I have never seen so many cute salt-and-pepper shaker sets in my entire life."

"Hey," said Jess, "I just remembered something! Next to the shoe store is one of those Everything-for-a-Dollar stores. They have some really wild salt-and-pepper sets in the window!"

---

34. Where does this story take place?

- (A) at a soccer field
- (B) in an antiques store
- (C) at Jess's home
- (D) at a tag sale

35. Which adjective best characterizes Jess?

- (A) determined
- (B) bad-tempered
- (C) selfish
- (D) greedy

36. The main purpose of this passage is to –

- (A) persuade
- (C) entertain
- (B) inform
- (D) explain

37. Jess solves her problem by –

- (A) buying cleats at a tag sale
- (B) making her mother feel guilty
- (C) combining her mother's wishes with her own
- (D) playing a trick on her mother

38. Jess's mother goes to many tag sales because she –

- (A) thinks that Jess enjoys them
- (B) buys things for her antique store
- (C) wants Jess to work for her
- (D) does not enjoy soccer games

Stop

Pretest

LANGUAGE ARTS: Mechanics and Usage

Directions: Read each sentence and look at the underlined word or words. Look for a mistake in capitalization, punctuation, or word usage. If you find a mistake, choose the best way to write the underlined part of the sentence. If there is no mistake, fill in the bubble beside answer D, "Correct as is."

1. Tyler <u>goed</u> running before school.

   Ⓐ going   Ⓒ gone
   Ⓑ went   Ⓓ Correct as is

2. The ship <u>had sank</u>, but all the passengers were rescued.

   Ⓐ is sinking   Ⓒ sank
   Ⓑ will sink   Ⓓ Correct as is

3. The twins asked for cake, so Mary gave some to <u>they</u>.

   Ⓐ them   Ⓒ their
   Ⓑ him   Ⓓ Correct as is

4. That soup tastes <u>really</u> delicious.

   Ⓐ real   Ⓒ realest
   Ⓑ realer   Ⓓ Correct as is

5. Either Juan <u>and</u> Holden borrowed my notebook last week.

   Ⓐ but   Ⓒ or
   Ⓑ nor   Ⓓ Correct as is

6. That was the <u>wonderfuller</u> trip ever!

   Ⓐ most wonderful
   Ⓑ wonderfullest
   Ⓒ more wonderful
   Ⓓ Correct as is

7. He <u>has never</u> sold a painting.

   Ⓐ hasn't never   Ⓒ has not never
   Ⓑ has ever   Ⓓ Correct as is

8. The letter was mailed <u>July 25 1996 from spain</u>.

   Ⓐ July 25 1996, from Spain
   Ⓑ July 25, 1996, from spain
   Ⓒ July 25, 1996, from Spain
   Ⓓ Correct as is

9. <u>"Aubrey</u> take your coat," said Mom.

   Ⓐ "Aubrey'   Ⓒ "Aubrey,
   Ⓑ "Aubrey: Ⓓ Correct as is

10. Cristina packed the following <u>items:</u> a lunchbag, two books, and an umbrella.

    Ⓐ items.   Ⓒ items"
    Ⓑ items,   Ⓓ Correct as is

11. The kids acted out <u>*Green eggs and ham*</u>.

    Ⓐ *Green Eggs And Ham*
    Ⓑ *Green Eggs and ham*
    Ⓒ *Green Eggs and Ham*
    Ⓓ Correct as is

Go On

LANGUAGE ARTS: Mechanics and Usage (continued)

Directions: Read the sentences. Find the underlined word that has a mistake in spelling. If there are no mistakes in spelling, fill in the bubble beside answer D, "No mistake."

12. Ⓐ Allegra was feeling <u>miserible</u>.
    Ⓑ She had to <u>memorize</u> a poem.
    Ⓒ The poem was about <u>shepherds</u>.
    Ⓓ No mistake

13. Ⓐ We walked by an old <u>cemetery</u>.
    Ⓑ It had an air of <u>mystery</u>.
    Ⓒ Everyone felt <u>frightened</u>.
    Ⓓ No mistake

14. Ⓐ The <u>governor</u> gave a speech.
    Ⓑ Her subject was the <u>enviroment</u>.
    Ⓒ She said it is <u>necessary</u> to protect the earth.
    Ⓓ No mistake

15. Ⓐ Kelly's sister causes <u>trubble</u>.
    Ⓑ She put mustard on my <u>glasses</u>.
    Ⓒ She shredded a <u>bouquet</u>.
    Ⓓ No mistake

16. Ⓐ Uncle Craig earns a big <u>salary</u>.
    Ⓑ He lives in an <u>apartment</u>.
    Ⓒ He drives a <u>forein</u> car.
    Ⓓ No mistake

17. Ⓐ Rona started her own <u>company</u>.
    Ⓑ She makes <u>kitchen</u> utensils.
    Ⓒ She carves <u>wooden</u> spoons.
    Ⓓ No mistake

Directions: Find the answer that is a complete sentence written correctly.

18. Ⓐ A crisp, sunny autumn day.
    Ⓑ We raked leaves we burned them.
    Ⓒ A large stack of pumpkins for sale.
    Ⓓ The weather report warned of frost that night.

19. Ⓐ Music poured out of the building.
    Ⓑ The lively sound of rattles, whistles, and drums.
    Ⓒ A dance school on the top floor.
    Ⓓ Teaching many different types of dance.

20. Ⓐ Mara gave a report it was about ancient Egypt.
    Ⓑ Explained how tombs were built.
    Ⓒ Pyramids filled with treasures.
    Ⓓ Egyptians wrote with symbols called hieroglyphics.

21. Ⓐ An alarm going off again.
    Ⓑ Elizabeth will be late for school.
    Ⓒ Eating breakfast and trying to find her backpack.
    Ⓓ At the corner, the school bus.

22. Ⓐ Dad made a piñata he filled it with toys.
    Ⓑ The first one to swing the bat.
    Ⓒ All the toys fell out.
    Ⓓ Children scrambling to pick up the toys.

Stop

Pretest

LANGUAGE ARTS: Composition

Directions: Read each paragraph. Then answer the questions that follow.

Paragraph 1

You don't have to play a sport or take up jogging with your parents. You can do simple things, such as volunteering to take the dog for a brisk walk every day after school. Maybe you can walk to school instead of taking the bus. You can walk to school instead of hitching a ride with your parents. You can do a few sit-ups and push-ups daily, even in the smallest apartment.

---

23. What is the best topic sentence for this paragraph?

Ⓐ Not all young people were born to be champion athletes.

Ⓑ Get up to change TV channels instead of using the remote!

Ⓒ There are many simple ways for young people to get into shape.

Ⓓ Studies show that many young people are unhealthy.

24. Which is the best way to combine the third and fourth sentences?

Ⓐ Maybe you can walk to school or hitch a ride with your parents instead of taking the bus.

Ⓑ Maybe you can walk to school instead of hitching a ride or taking the bus with your parents.

Ⓒ Instead of hitching a ride on the bus or with your parents, maybe you can walk to school.

Ⓓ Maybe you can walk to school instead of taking the bus or hitching a ride with your parents.

25. Which sentence would fit best at the end of this paragraph?

Ⓐ There is one best sport for everyone.

Ⓑ Your dog will be healthier and better behaved with frequent exercise.

Ⓒ Getting in shape will make you feel so much better.

Ⓓ Parents get really tired of driving their children everywhere.

26. This paragraph was probably written for what audience?

Ⓐ teachers

Ⓑ doctors

Ⓒ parents

Ⓓ young people

Go On →

Paragraph 2

Plastic is a useful building material because it does not rot the way wood does. Plastic is useful in buildings because it does not rust like metal. When plastic is first made, it is hot and stretchable. This makes it possible to form into almost any shape a manufacturer might need. Plastics were invented about sixty years ago. Electricity cannot pass through plastic. Therefore, plastic is a useful material for covering over electrical wire because it is a safe covering.

---

27. What is the best topic sentence for this paragraph?

Ⓐ People should try to recycle their plastics.

Ⓑ Plastic has many useful characteristics.

Ⓒ Plastic is made from a variety of chemicals.

Ⓓ There are two main types of plastics.

28. Which sentence does **not** belong in this paragraph?

Ⓐ Plastic is useful in buildings because it does not rust like metal.

Ⓑ This makes it possible to form into almost any shape a manufacturer might need.

Ⓒ Plastics were invented about sixty years ago.

Ⓓ Electricity cannot pass through plastic.

29. Which is the best way to combine the first two sentences?

Ⓐ Plastic is a useful building material because it does not rot like wood or rust like metal.

Ⓑ Plastic is a useful building material because it does not rot like metal or wood.

Ⓒ Plastic is a useful building material and it does not rot and also it does not rust.

Ⓓ Plastic unlike wood which rots and metal which rusts is a useful building material, because it does not.

30. Which is the best way to revise the last sentence?

Ⓐ Therefore, it is safe to use plastic to cover wire because it is useful.

Ⓑ Therefore, safely cover all wiring with plastic.

Ⓒ Therefore, safety rules show that it is safe to use plastic as a wire cover.

Ⓓ Therefore, plastic is a safe covering for electrical wire.

Stop

Pretest

LANGUAGE ARTS: Study Skills

Directions: Choose the best answer to each question about finding information.

31. If you wanted to find information on yesterday's sports events, you should look in –

Ⓐ a newspaper

Ⓑ an atlas

Ⓒ an encyclopedia

Ⓓ a thesaurus

32. To find a synonym for a word used in your writing, you should look in –

Ⓐ an index

Ⓑ an encyclopedia

Ⓒ a thesaurus

Ⓓ an atlas

33. To find a book about General Lafayette, a hero of the American Revolution, you should look in an online library catalog under –

Ⓐ General Ⓒ American

Ⓑ Lafayette Ⓓ Revolution

34. Which word would come first in alphabetical order?

Ⓐ heave Ⓒ heather

Ⓑ heavily Ⓓ hearty

35. Which of these is a main heading that includes the other topics?

Ⓐ Government Ⓒ Cabinet

Ⓑ President Ⓓ Congress

Use the dictionary entry to answer questions 36–38.

> **pot•pour•ri** (pō' pŏŏ rē') *n.* **1.** A fragrant mixture of spices and dried flowers. **2.** Any mixture or grouping of miscellaneous things.
>
> **pouf** (pŏŏf) *n.* **1.** A high, old-fashioned headdress. **2.** Any puffed up part of a dress.
>
> **poul•tice** (pōl' tis) *n.* A moist, warm substance put on wounds to soothe or cure them.
>
> ### Pronunciation Guide
>
> | | |
> |---|---|
> | ē as in me | ŏŏ as in book |
> | i as in it | ōō as in soon |
> | ō as in hope | ou as in pound |

36. The *o* in *pouf* is pronounced like the *o* in –

Ⓐ hope Ⓒ soon

Ⓑ book Ⓓ pound

37. How many syllables are there in *potpourri?*

Ⓐ 2 Ⓒ 4

Ⓑ 3 Ⓓ 5

38. A *poultice* is a kind of –

Ⓐ fragrant mixture

Ⓑ fashionable hat

Ⓒ clothing

Ⓓ medical treatment

11

Stop

Pretest

MATHEMATICS: Concepts and Applications

Directions: Choose the best answer to each question.

1. $600,000 + 2000 + 800 + 30 =$

   (A) 620,830
   (C) 62,830
   (B) 628,030
   (D) 602,830

2. Which is another way to express $7 \times 7 \times 7$?

   (A) 3×7
   (C) 7^3
   (B) $7 + 3$
   (D) 3^7

3. What is the value of **2** in 72,960?

   (A) 2 ten thousands
   (B) 2 thousands
   (C) 2 hundreds
   (D) 2 tens

4. What is 3846 rounded to the nearest ten?

   (A) 4000
   (C) 3850
   (B) 3900
   (D) 3840

5. What fraction of this square is shaded?

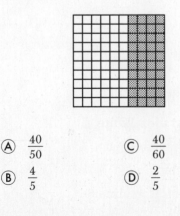

   (A) $\frac{40}{50}$
   (C) $\frac{40}{60}$
   (B) $\frac{4}{5}$
   (D) $\frac{2}{5}$

6. Lourdes is making a necklace with a regular pattern of blue and yellow beads. The necklace begins with 5 blue, 3 yellow; next 7 blue, 4 yellow; and then 10 blue, 6 yellow. What would come next?

   (A) 13 blue, 8 yellow
   (B) 7 blue, 3 yellow
   (C) 14 blue, 9 yellow
   (D) 20 blue, 12 yellow

7. Which lists all the factors of 8?

   (A) 1, 8
   (C) 2, 4, 6
   (B) 3, 5
   (D) 1, 2, 4, 8

8. Which number sentence is true?

   (A) $^-9 = 9$
   (C) $^-9 > 9$
   (B) $^-9 > 0$
   (D) $^-9 < 9$

9. What is an equivalent fraction for $\frac{12}{16}$?

   (A) $\frac{4}{3}$
   (C) $\frac{6}{7}$
   (B) $\frac{3}{4}$
   (D) $\frac{2}{3}$

10. Which fraction is least?

   (A) $\frac{3}{9}$
   (C) $\frac{1}{5}$
   (B) $\frac{2}{3}$
   (D) $\frac{6}{12}$

Go On

MATHEMATICS: Concepts and Applications (continued)

11. Which decimal number has the same value as $\frac{3}{5}$?

   Ⓐ 0.5

   Ⓑ 0.6

   Ⓒ 0.15

   Ⓓ 1.5

12. Which number is greatest?

   Ⓐ 0.124

   Ⓑ 0.056

   Ⓒ 0.009

   Ⓓ 0.263

13. The **8** in 4.768 represents –

   Ⓐ 8 thousandths

   Ⓑ 8 hundredths

   Ⓒ 8 tenths

   Ⓓ 8 ones

14. What is 6.257 rounded to the nearest tenth?

   Ⓐ 6.26

   Ⓑ 6.2

   Ⓒ 6.3

   Ⓓ 6.0

15. The arrow points to what number on the number line?

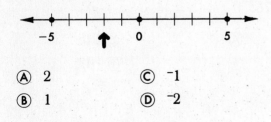

   Ⓐ 2   Ⓒ ⁻1

   Ⓑ 1   Ⓓ ⁻2

16. Which number goes in the circle to make this sentence true?

$$(49 \times 71) \times 6 = \bigcirc \times (71 \times 6)$$

   Ⓐ 6   Ⓒ 49

   Ⓑ 12   Ⓓ 71

17. Which point on the grid represents (4, 0)?

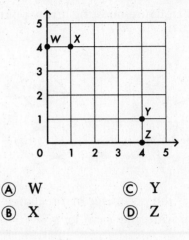

   Ⓐ W   Ⓒ Y

   Ⓑ X   Ⓓ Z

18. What is the radius of a circle with a diameter of 8 inches?

   Ⓐ 2 in.   Ⓒ 12 in.

   Ⓑ 4 in.   Ⓓ 16 in.

19. Which is a right angle?

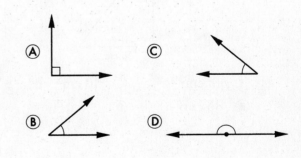

Go On

20. Which figure shows a reflection of 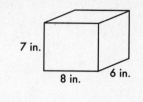 ?

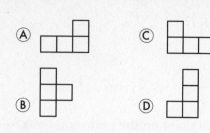

Ⓐ   Ⓒ
Ⓑ   Ⓓ

21. In which figure does the arrow point to a vertex?

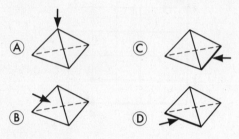

Ⓐ   Ⓒ
Ⓑ   Ⓓ

22. What is the perimeter of a rectangle that is 4 cm wide and 7 cm long?

Ⓐ 11 cm   Ⓒ 22 cm
Ⓑ 14 cm   Ⓓ 28 cm

23. What is the area of the triangle?

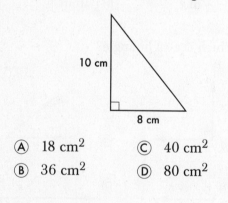

Ⓐ 18 cm^2 Ⓒ 40 cm^2
Ⓑ 36 cm^2 Ⓓ 80 cm^2

24. What is the volume of the rectangular prism?

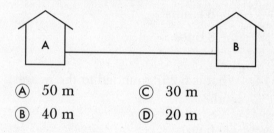

Ⓐ 21 in.^{3} Ⓒ 168 in.^{3}
Ⓑ 55 in.^{3} Ⓓ 336 in.^{3}

25. Ali's piano lesson began at 3:15. It ended at 4:05. How long did the lesson last?

Ⓐ 45 min   Ⓒ 55 min
Ⓑ 50 min   Ⓓ 1 hour

26. In the figure below, what is the approximate distance from House A to House B? The scale is 1 cm = 5 m.

Ⓐ 50 m   Ⓒ 30 m
Ⓑ 40 m   Ⓓ 20 m

27. Josefina's room is $3\frac{2}{3}$ yd long. How many feet is that?

Ⓐ 9 ft   Ⓒ 11 ft
Ⓑ 10 ft   Ⓓ 12 ft

28. If $28 - n = 16$, what is n?

Ⓐ 12   Ⓒ 16
Ⓑ 14   Ⓓ 44

Go On

MATHEMATICS: Concepts and Applications (continued)

Directions: Solve each problem. If the correct answer is Not Given, mark answer D, "NG."

29. Matt makes between $28.00 and $32.00 each Sunday on his paper route. <u>About</u> how many Sundays would it take for him to make $300.00?

   Ⓐ 5   Ⓒ 15

   Ⓑ 10   Ⓓ 20

30. Arnie has 5 T-shirts and 3 pairs of shorts. How many different outfits of 1 T-shirt and 1 pair of shorts can he make?

   Ⓐ 8   Ⓒ 15

   Ⓑ 10   Ⓓ NG

Use the line graph below to answer 31–32.

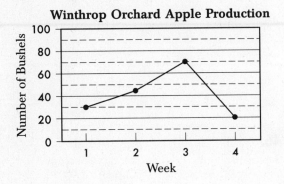

Winthrop Orchard Apple Production

31. In which week were the most bushels of apples picked?

   Ⓐ Week 1   Ⓒ Week 3

   Ⓑ Week 2   Ⓓ Week 4

32. How many more bushels of apples were picked in Week 2 than in Week 4?

   Ⓐ 10   Ⓒ 20

   Ⓑ 15   Ⓓ NG

33. There are 3 shrimp puffs, 7 miniature hot dogs, 8 pineapple wedges, and 6 stuffed tomatoes on a plate of appetizers. If Kim takes one appetizer without looking, what is the probability that she will pick a stuffed tomato?

   Ⓐ $\frac{1}{4}$ Ⓒ $\frac{5}{24}$

   Ⓑ $\frac{1}{6}$ Ⓓ NG

34. The 16 members of the Drama Club want to go to a play for which the tickets cost $6.50 each. To raise money, the students wash 23 cars at $3.00 per car. How much more money do they need to raise?

   Ⓐ $25.00   Ⓒ $81.00

   Ⓑ $35.00   Ⓓ NG

35. In Clay's class, 2 out of 3 students usually buy lunch instead of bringing lunch. If there are 18 students in Clay's class, how many usually buy lunch?

   Ⓐ 9   Ⓒ 12

   Ⓑ 10   Ⓓ NG

36. Amanda invited 8 friends to her party, but 2 got sick and couldn't come. Amanda spent $1.85 on a party bag for each friend who came. Which number sentence should be used to find how much she spent?

   Ⓐ $(8 - 2) \times \$1.85 = \square$

   Ⓑ $8 \times (2 - \$1.85) = \square$

   Ⓒ $(8 \times \$1.85) - 2 = \square$

   Ⓓ $8 - 2 + \$1.85 = \square$

Stop

Pretest

MATHEMATICS: Computation

Directions: Find the answer to each problem. If the correct answer is not given, mark answer D, "None of these."

37. $8644 - 2957 =$

 (A) 5687
 (B) 6797
 (C) 11,601
 (D) None of these

38. $490 \times 100 =$

 (A) 0.490
 (B) 4900
 (C) 49,000
 (D) None of these

39. $\begin{array}{r} 264 \\ \times\ 47 \\ \hline \end{array}$

 (A) 12,488
 (B) 12,418
 (C) 12,388
 (D) None of these

40. $7\overline{)409}$

 (A) 70
 (B) 58 R3
 (C) 58
 (D) None of these

41. $7.54 + 2.39 =$

 (A) 7.779
 (B) 9.92
 (C) 9.93
 (D) None of these

42. $0.8 \times 0.6 =$

 (A) 4.8
 (B) 0.48
 (C) 0.048
 (D) None of these

43. $\begin{array}{r} 3\frac{5}{6} \\ +\ 2\frac{1}{6} \\ \hline \end{array}$

 (A) $1\frac{2}{3}$
 (B) $5\frac{2}{3}$
 (C) $6\frac{1}{6}$
 (D) None of these

44. $\begin{array}{r} \$221.63 \\ -\ 13.87 \\ \hline \end{array}$

 (A) $82.93
 (B) $207.13
 (C) $235.50
 (D) None of these

45. $5\overline{)1.85}$

 (A) 0.37
 (B) 3.7
 (C) 37
 (D) None of these

46. $\frac{3}{4} + \frac{1}{2} =$

 (A) 1
 (B) $1\frac{1}{6}$
 (C) $1\frac{1}{4}$
 (D) None of these

47. $\frac{1}{8} \times \frac{4}{5} =$

 (A) $\frac{5}{40}$
 (B) $\frac{1}{10}$
 (C) $\frac{4}{20}$
 (D) None of these

48. $\frac{5}{8} \div \frac{3}{16} =$

 (A) $\frac{15}{128}$
 (B) $3\frac{1}{3}$
 (C) $\frac{20}{8}$
 (D) None of these

Stop

Reading

PRACTICE 1 • Synonyms and Antonyms

SAMPLES

Directions: Choose the word that means the same, or almost the same, as the underlined word.

A. a nice <u>mural</u>

   Ⓐ color   Ⓒ brush

   Ⓑ painting   Ⓓ rainbow

Directions: Choose the word that means the OPPOSITE of the underlined word.

B. to <u>originate</u>

   Ⓐ start   Ⓒ finish

   Ⓑ build   Ⓓ improve

Tips and Reminders

- When looking for a synonym, watch out for answer choices that are related to the underlined word but have different meanings.

- When looking for an antonym, watch out for words that have the same meaning (such as *originate* and *start*).

PRACTICE

Directions: Choose the word that means the same, or almost the same, as the underlined word.

1. the <u>outcome</u>

   Ⓐ cause

   Ⓑ beginning

   Ⓒ victory

   Ⓓ result

2. to <u>interpret</u>

   Ⓐ punish

   Ⓑ translate

   Ⓒ measure

   Ⓓ search

3. a <u>majestic</u> home

   Ⓐ grand

   Ⓑ humble

   Ⓒ poor

   Ⓓ mean

4. a large <u>quantity</u>

   Ⓐ person

   Ⓑ brand

   Ⓒ amount

   Ⓓ company

Go On

5. will <u>accuse</u>

  Ⓐ attempt

  Ⓑ blame

  Ⓒ confuse

  Ⓓ deny

6. to <u>detect</u>

  Ⓐ forgive

  Ⓑ leave

  Ⓒ whisper

  Ⓓ discover

7. a <u>flimsy</u> excuse

  Ⓐ true

  Ⓑ short

  Ⓒ weak

  Ⓓ likely

8. same <u>instructor</u>

  Ⓐ teacher

  Ⓑ worker

  Ⓒ actor

  Ⓓ stranger

9. will <u>astound</u>

  Ⓐ satisfy

  Ⓑ amaze

  Ⓒ please

  Ⓓ attract

10. extremely <u>rigid</u>

  Ⓐ content

  Ⓑ violent

  Ⓒ stiff

  Ⓓ shabby

11. very <u>serene</u>

  Ⓐ calm

  Ⓑ awake

  Ⓒ bashful

  Ⓓ shrewd

12. to <u>vibrate</u>

  Ⓐ control

  Ⓑ regard

  Ⓒ permit

  Ⓓ shake

13. great <u>monarch</u>

  Ⓐ athlete

  Ⓑ treasure

  Ⓒ ruler

  Ⓓ throne

14. quick <u>inspection</u>

  Ⓐ experiment

  Ⓑ imagination

  Ⓒ examination

  Ⓓ decision

15. new <u>parka</u>

  Ⓐ coat

  Ⓑ job

  Ⓒ chance

  Ⓓ opening

16. will <u>reject</u>

  Ⓐ approve

  Ⓑ refuse

  Ⓒ threaten

  Ⓓ resume

Go On

PRACTICE 1 • Synonyms and Antonyms (continued)

Directions: Choose the word that means the OPPOSITE of the underlined word.

17. was <u>temporary</u>
    - Ⓐ brief
    - Ⓑ gradual
    - Ⓒ recent
    - Ⓓ permanent

18. is <u>carefree</u>
    - Ⓐ wild
    - Ⓑ troubled
    - Ⓒ prompt
    - Ⓓ clumsy

19. <u>elevate</u> slightly
    - Ⓐ lower
    - Ⓑ delay
    - Ⓒ shorten
    - Ⓓ raise

20. sudden <u>weakness</u>
    - Ⓐ kindness
    - Ⓑ fearfulness
    - Ⓒ despair
    - Ⓓ strength

21. something <u>minor</u>
    - Ⓐ small
    - Ⓑ modest
    - Ⓒ major
    - Ⓓ definite

22. was <u>hostile</u>
    - Ⓐ angry
    - Ⓑ friendly
    - Ⓒ unkind
    - Ⓓ jealous

23. in <u>chaos</u>
    - Ⓐ order
    - Ⓑ pleasure
    - Ⓒ agony
    - Ⓓ confusion

24. to <u>oppose</u>
    - Ⓐ value
    - Ⓑ abandon
    - Ⓒ support
    - Ⓓ resist

25. abrupt <u>departure</u>
    - Ⓐ arrival
    - Ⓑ release
    - Ⓒ ending
    - Ⓓ retreat

26. extremely <u>vague</u>
    - Ⓐ pale
    - Ⓑ honest
    - Ⓒ sturdy
    - Ⓓ clear

27. quite <u>ambitious</u>
    - Ⓐ hopeful
    - Ⓑ depressed
    - Ⓒ lazy
    - Ⓓ artistic

28. was <u>complex</u>
    - Ⓐ single
    - Ⓑ difficult
    - Ⓒ unusual
    - Ⓓ simple

Stop

Language Arts

PRACTICE 2 • Using Verbs

Directions: Read each sentence and look at the underlined word or words. There may be a mistake in word usage. If you find a mistake, choose the best way to write the underlined part of the sentence. If there is no mistake, fill in the bubble beside answer D, "Correct as is."

SAMPLES

A. Yesterday he <u>builded</u> a bird feeder.

    Ⓐ builds   Ⓒ building

    Ⓑ built   Ⓓ Correct as is

B. Eileen and Jason <u>will be</u> late.

    Ⓐ was   Ⓒ been

    Ⓑ is   Ⓓ Correct as is

Tips and Reminders

- Try each answer choice in the sentence to see which one sounds right.

- Be careful with irregular forms of verbs, such as *built* and *been.*

- Watch out for incorrect forms of words, such as *builded.*

PRACTICE

1. Kirsten and Lindsey <u>is picking</u> apples.

    Ⓐ was picking

    Ⓑ are picking

    Ⓒ has been picking

    Ⓓ Correct as is

2. Jill <u>hasn't being</u> in class all week.

    Ⓐ haven't being

    Ⓑ wasn't being

    Ⓒ hasn't been

    Ⓓ Correct as is

3. <u>Have you heared</u> a weather report?

    Ⓐ Has you heard

    Ⓑ Have you hearing

    Ⓒ Have you heard

    Ⓓ Correct as is

4. One of those hats <u>is</u> mine.

    Ⓐ are

    Ⓑ were

    Ⓒ be

    Ⓓ Correct as is

Go On →

5. Both of us <u>love</u> ice cream.

(A) loves

(B) is loving

(C) has loved

(D) Correct as is

6. Nate <u>have outgrown</u> most of his clothes by next summer.

(A) has outgrew

(B) will have outgrown

(C) outgrowed

(D) Correct as is

7. The girls <u>scream</u> when lightning hit the tree.

(A) screaming

(B) was screaming

(C) screamed

(D) Correct as is

8. Our family <u>drived</u> to Maine last week.

(A) will be driving

(B) drove

(C) drives

(D) Correct as is

9. Casey's dad <u>learned</u> him how to skate.

(A) teached

(B) is learning

(C) taught

(D) Correct as is

10. Only a few of the dogs we saw at the animal shelter <u>was</u> puppies.

(A) were

(B) will be

(C) is

(D) Correct as is

11. The stormy weather <u>keeped</u> everyone inside.

(A) keep

(B) keeping

(C) kept

(D) Correct as is

12. That woman <u>looking</u> familiar.

(A) look

(B) looks

(C) are looking

(D) Correct as is

13. The flower pot <u>must have falled</u> off the porch.

(A) must have felled

(B) must have fallen

(C) must have fall

(D) Correct as is

14. Jenna <u>tried to hurry</u>, but she still missed the bus.

(A) tries to hurry

(B) trying to hurry

(C) will try to hurry

(D) Correct as is

Stop

Mathematics

PRACTICE 3 • Whole Number Concepts

Directions: Choose the best answer to each question.

SAMPLES

A. $30{,}000 + 5000 + 200 + 7 =$

   (A) 305,207   (C) 35,270

   (B) 30,527   (D) 35,207

B. Which is another way to express $8 \times 8 \times 8$?

   (A) 8^3 (C) 3^8

   (B) 8×3 (D) $3 \times (8 + 8)$

C. What is 6872 rounded to the nearest 100?

   (A) 7000   (C) 6870

   (B) 6900   (D) 6800

D. Which lists all the factors of 14?

   (A) 2, 7   (C) 1, 2, 7, 14

   (B) 1, 14   (D) 1, 2, 14, 28

Tips and Reminders

- Be sure to look at all the answer choices before you choose an answer. Try each answer choice to find the one that is correct.

- After choosing an answer, read the question again to make sure you have answered it correctly.

PRACTICE

1. Which number means two million one hundred forty-five thousand three hundred twenty?

   (A) 245,320

   (B) 2,145,320

   (C) 214,532

   (D) 21,450,320

2. What is the value of the **7** in 374,260?

   (A) 70

   (B) 700

   (C) 7000

   (D) 70,000

Go On

3. Which is an even number?

Ⓐ 645   Ⓒ 482
Ⓑ 517   Ⓓ 239

4. $4^3 =$

Ⓐ 64   Ⓒ 16
Ⓑ 48   Ⓓ 12

5. What is 8923 rounded to the nearest 100?

Ⓐ 9000   Ⓒ 8920
Ⓑ 8900   Ⓓ 8000

6. Which number comes next?

3, 9, 27, 81, ___?___ , . . .

Ⓐ 90   Ⓒ 153
Ⓑ 108   Ⓓ 243

7. Which sentence is true?

Ⓐ $^-5 < 0$ Ⓒ $^-5 = 5$
Ⓑ $0 < ^-5$ Ⓓ $^-5 > 5$

8. If the **8** in 9482 is changed to a **4**, how is the value of the number changed?

Ⓐ The number increases by 80.
Ⓑ The number increases by 40.
Ⓒ The number decreases by 80.
Ⓓ The number decreases by 40.

9. Which number could go in the box to make the sentence true?

$^-12 < \square < 12$

Ⓐ 15   Ⓒ $^-13$
Ⓑ $^-1$ Ⓓ $^-24$

10. Which is a factor of 121?

Ⓐ 5   Ⓒ 9
Ⓑ 7   Ⓓ 11

11. A number machine spits out the numbers 8, 4, 0, $^-4$, ... Which number comes next?

Ⓐ 0   Ⓒ 4
Ⓑ $^-8$ Ⓓ $^-6$

12. Which number is greater than 3479 but less than 3742?

Ⓐ 3456   Ⓒ 3572
Ⓑ 3468   Ⓓ 3751

13. Which is another way to write 5×5?

Ⓐ 5^2
Ⓑ 2^5
Ⓒ $(5 \times 2) + (5 \times 2)$
Ⓓ 5×2

14. $10,000 + 600 + 70 + 3 =$

Ⓐ 106,703   Ⓒ 16,073
Ⓑ 16,730   Ⓓ 10,673

Reading

PRACTICE 4 • Context Clues

SAMPLES

Directions: Read the sentences. Choose the word that best completes both sentences.

A. Marla swept the sand away from the fossil with a small _____.
Mrs. Pickens hired me to clear the _____ from her yard.

  Ⓐ broom

  Ⓑ grass

  Ⓒ tool

  Ⓓ brush

Directions: Read the sentences. Choose the word that best fits in the blank.

    Mr. Carey lost control of his car. He barely avoided a __(B)__ with another vehicle.

B. Ⓐ race

  Ⓑ collision

  Ⓒ nudge

  Ⓓ meeting

Tips and Reminders

• Think of the different meanings you know for each word. Watch out for words that fit one sentence but not the other.

• Read the whole paragraph first. Try each answer choice in the sentence to see which one sounds right.

PRACTICE

Directions: Read the sentences. Choose the word that best completes both sentences.

1. How did you _____ your ankle?
Peter used a _____ to loosen the bolt.

  Ⓐ break

  Ⓑ twist

  Ⓒ hammer

  Ⓓ wrench

2. The umpire decided to _____ the game when snow began to fall.
Help me _____ this lamp from the ceiling.

  Ⓐ suspend

  Ⓑ detach

  Ⓒ instruct

  Ⓓ dangle

Go On →

3. The _____ of the storm has not yet been determined.
   The glass shattered on _____ when it hit the floor.

   Ⓐ direction

   Ⓑ impact

   Ⓒ pressure

   Ⓓ instinct

4. This computer came with a one-year _____.
   I'll invite him, but I can't _____ that he'll show up.

   Ⓐ guarantee

   Ⓑ supply

   Ⓒ promise

   Ⓓ expect

5. Suzi hid the TV's _____ control.
   The camp was located in a _____ area in Maine.

   Ⓐ distant

   Ⓑ quality

   Ⓒ remote

   Ⓓ barren

6. The dentist found a _____ in Sally's tooth.
   The animal hid in a small _____ formed by two rocks.

   Ⓐ cave

   Ⓑ filling

   Ⓒ cavity

   Ⓓ crumb

7. Melissa earns a decent _____ for babysitting.
   The students at our school have decided to _____ a war against drugs.

   Ⓐ start

   Ⓑ wage

   Ⓒ profit

   Ⓓ schedule

8. Josie attended her sister's wedding _____.
   I'm getting very poor _____ from this new radio.

   Ⓐ ceremony

   Ⓑ reception

   Ⓒ performance

   Ⓓ selection

9. Someone broke into the bank's _____.
   Watch me _____ over this fence!

   Ⓐ safe

   Ⓑ launch

   Ⓒ register

   Ⓓ vault

10. Gary climbed to the top of the _____.
    Jane tried to _____ her way through the interview, but she was not qualified for the job.

    Ⓐ bluff

    Ⓑ peak

    Ⓒ mound

    Ⓓ fake

Go On

Directions: Read each paragraph. Then choose the word that best fits in each numbered blank.

A sudden snowstorm resulted in early __(11)__ of students in most area schools. Students were __(12)__ to go directly home on the buses provided. Even the school __(13)__ left early. A weather forecaster __(14)__ that we would have at least a foot of snow by nightfall. As a result, all after-school activities were canceled.

---

11. Ⓐ applause
    Ⓑ recess
    Ⓒ arrival
    Ⓓ dismissal

12. Ⓐ offended
    Ⓑ instructed
    Ⓒ threatened
    Ⓓ revised

13. Ⓐ custodians
    Ⓑ physicians
    Ⓒ lawyers
    Ⓓ candidates

14. Ⓐ observed
    Ⓑ patterned
    Ⓒ discussed
    Ⓓ predicted

When the __(15)__ rode into town, his plan was to rob the stagecoach that would soon arrive. Then he spotted the sheriff over by the jail. The would-be thief quickly __(16)__ his plans for a robbery and __(17)__ his horse forward. He rode hard until he reached the __(18)__ of town where the rest of his gang was waiting for him.

---

15. Ⓐ army
    Ⓑ outlaw
    Ⓒ athlete
    Ⓓ carriage

16. Ⓐ cashed
    Ⓑ recalled
    Ⓒ abandoned
    Ⓓ dared

17. Ⓐ urged
    Ⓑ pulled
    Ⓒ ruled
    Ⓓ reined

18. Ⓐ fortress
    Ⓑ outskirts
    Ⓒ battlefield
    Ⓓ wilderness

Stop

Language Arts

PRACTICE 5 • Grammar and Usage

Directions: Read each passage. The underlined parts may contain mistakes in word usage. Choose the best way to write each underlined part. If it contains no mistakes, choose answer D, "as it is."

SAMPLES

> Katie and me were planning to go to the movies. Katie phoned to say they
>   **(A)**   **(B)**
> couldn't go, so I went with Chris instead. We saw the funnier movie we've
>   **(C)**
> ever seen. I hope I don't ever laugh that hard again!
>   **(D)**

A. In sentence A, Katie and me is best written –

    Ⓐ Me and Katie

    Ⓑ I and Katie

    Ⓒ Katie and I

    Ⓓ as it is

C. In sentence C, funnier movie is best written –

    Ⓐ funniest movie

    Ⓑ funniest movie

    Ⓒ most funniest movie

    Ⓓ as it is

B. In sentence B, they couldn't go is best written –

    Ⓐ she couldn't go

    Ⓑ it couldn't go

    Ⓒ us couldn't go

    Ⓓ as it is

D. In sentence D, don't ever laugh is best written –

    Ⓐ don't never laugh

    Ⓑ don't not ever laugh

    Ⓒ do never laugh

    Ⓓ as it is

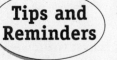

Tips and Reminders

• Try each answer choice in the sentence to see which one sounds right.

• Watch out for incorrect forms of words, such as *funnierest*.

Go On

PRACTICE 5 • Grammar and Usage (continued)

PRACTICE

Are you looking for a pet that <u>is friendliest</u> than most animals and easy to
 (1)

care for? If so, a hamster may be the perfect pet <u>for yours</u>. Hamsters are
 (2) (3)

solitary creatures. <u>Them</u> would almost rather be alone. It's alright to get more
 (4) (5)

than one hamster, <u>yet</u> be prepared to provide a cage for each one of them.

<u>Neither cardboard nor wood</u> should be used for a cage. Metal <u>works goodest</u>
 (6) (7)

because a hamster can't chew through metal and get free. Whatever you do,
 (8)

<u>don't never ever</u> let a hamster run around free in your house. A hamster on
 (9)

the loose can change from pet to pest <u>quicker</u> than you can blink an eye.

---

1. In sentence 1, <u>is friendliest</u> is best written –

 Ⓐ is friendly

 Ⓑ is friendlier

 Ⓒ is more friendlier

 Ⓓ as it is

2. In sentence 2, <u>for yours</u> is best written –

 Ⓐ for you   Ⓒ for yourself

 Ⓑ for your   Ⓓ as it is

3. In sentence 4, <u>Them</u> is best written –

 Ⓐ They   Ⓒ He

 Ⓑ It   Ⓓ as it is

4. In sentence 5, <u>yet</u> is best written –

 Ⓐ or

 Ⓑ because

 Ⓒ but

 Ⓓ as it is

5. In sentence 6, <u>Neither cardboard nor wood</u> is best written –

 Ⓐ Neither cardboard or wood

 Ⓑ Neither cardboard and wood

 Ⓒ Neither cardboard but wood

 Ⓓ as it is

6. In sentence 7, <u>works goodest</u> is best written –

 Ⓐ works best   Ⓒ works gooder

 Ⓑ works bestest   Ⓓ as it is

7. In sentence 8, <u>don't never ever</u> is best written –

 Ⓐ don't never   Ⓒ don't not ever

 Ⓑ don't ever   Ⓓ as it is

8. In sentence 9, <u>quicker</u> is best written –

 Ⓐ quickest   Ⓒ quick

 Ⓑ more quicker   Ⓓ as it is

Mathematics

PRACTICE 6 • Fractions and Decimals

Directions: Choose the best answer to each question.

SAMPLES

A. Which fraction is equivalent to $\frac{8}{24}$?

  Ⓐ $\frac{1}{3}$

  Ⓑ $\frac{3}{4}$

  Ⓒ $\frac{4}{6}$

  Ⓓ $\frac{3}{12}$

B. What is 3.508 rounded to the nearest hundredth?

  Ⓐ 4.00

  Ⓑ 3.50

  Ⓒ 3.60

  Ⓓ 3.51

Tips and Reminders

- To compare fractions, change them to "like" fractions with the same denominator.
- To compare decimal numbers, line up the decimal points.

PRACTICE

1. What part of the fraction bars is shaded?

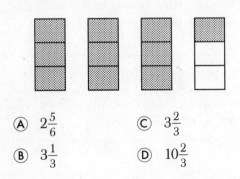

  Ⓐ $2\frac{5}{6}$ Ⓒ $3\frac{2}{3}$

  Ⓑ $3\frac{1}{3}$ Ⓓ $10\frac{2}{3}$

2. Which list shows the decimal numbers in order from least to greatest?

  Ⓐ 2.50, 2.05, 0.25, 0.025

  Ⓑ 2.05, 2.50, 0.025, 0.25

  Ⓒ 0.25, 0.025, 2.05, 2.50

  Ⓓ 0.025, 0.25, 2.05, 2.50

3. Which number sentence is true?

  Ⓐ $\frac{5}{25} = \frac{1}{5}$ Ⓒ $\frac{1}{2} > \frac{2}{3}$

  Ⓑ $\frac{3}{4} < \frac{1}{2}$ Ⓓ $\frac{5}{6} = 1\frac{1}{6}$

Go On

4. Which fraction is equivalent to $\frac{18}{20}$?

Ⓐ $\frac{6}{7}$ Ⓒ $\frac{9}{10}$

Ⓑ $\frac{4}{5}$ Ⓓ $\frac{3}{4}$

5. $\frac{9}{100}$ can be expressed as –

Ⓐ 0.009   Ⓒ 0.9

Ⓑ 0.09   Ⓓ 9.0

6. What part of the square is shaded?

Ⓐ $\frac{1}{4}$ Ⓒ $\frac{4}{5}$

Ⓑ $\frac{7}{10}$ Ⓓ $\frac{3}{4}$

7. Which number is least?

Ⓐ 8.415   Ⓒ 8.154

Ⓑ 8.514   Ⓓ 8.145

8. Which fraction is greatest?

Ⓐ $\frac{11}{15}$ Ⓒ $\frac{9}{10}$

Ⓑ $\frac{4}{5}$ Ⓓ $\frac{7}{8}$

9. What is the value of the 3 in 2.1347?

Ⓐ $\frac{3}{10}$ Ⓒ $\frac{3}{1000}$

Ⓑ $\frac{3}{100}$ Ⓓ $\frac{3}{10,000}$

10. What is 18.072 rounded to the nearest tenth?

Ⓐ 20.0   Ⓒ 18.1

Ⓑ 19.0   Ⓓ 18.0

11. $\frac{25}{6}$ can be expressed as –

Ⓐ $4\frac{1}{6}$ Ⓒ $3\frac{5}{6}$

Ⓑ $4\frac{2}{3}$ Ⓓ $3\frac{1}{6}$

12. Which decimal number has the greatest value?

Ⓐ 0.08   Ⓒ 0.80

Ⓑ 8.0   Ⓓ 80.0

13. If each 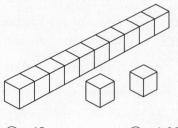 is 0.1, what number is shown in the figure below?

Ⓐ 12   Ⓒ 1.02

Ⓑ 0.12   Ⓓ 1.20

14. Which arrow points to 0.3 on the number line?

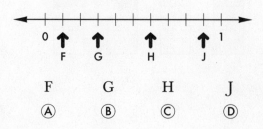

F   G   H   J

Ⓐ   Ⓑ   Ⓒ   Ⓓ

Stop

Reading

PRACTICE 7 • Word Analysis

SAMPLES

Directions: Choose the word or phrase that gives the meaning of the underlined prefix or suffix.

A. <u>non</u>fiction   <u>non</u>stop

   Ⓐ single
   Ⓑ not
   Ⓒ wrong
   Ⓓ before

B. natur<u>al</u>   roy<u>al</u>

   Ⓐ filled with
   Ⓑ opposite
   Ⓒ without
   Ⓓ related to

Directions: Read the sentence and the question. Choose the word that best answers the question.

C. The _____ children ate everything on their plates and asked for seconds. Which word would suggest extreme hunger?

   Ⓐ naughty   Ⓒ ravenous
   Ⓑ satisfied   Ⓓ greedy

Directions: Read the meaning of the original word. Then choose the modern word that comes from the original word.

D. Which word probably comes from the Latin word *infundere,* meaning "to pour in"?

   Ⓐ funnel   Ⓒ funny
   Ⓑ funeral   Ⓓ function

Tips and Reminders

- A prefix is a word part added to the beginning of a word, as in <u>un</u>like and <u>non</u>stop.

- A suffix is a word part added to the end of a word, as in *like<u>ness</u>* and *natur<u>al</u>*.

- The *connotation* of a word is the meaning that it suggests. To find the correct connotation, think about the suggested meaning of each word.

- To find the modern word that comes from an original word, look carefully at the spelling of each answer choice and think about what it means.

Go On

PRACTICE

Directions: Choose the word or phrase that gives the meaning of the underlined prefix or suffix.

1. <u>mis</u>understood   <u>mis</u>lead

   (A) of or like
   (B) wrongly
   (C) having
   (D) remove from

2. <u>fore</u>see   <u>fore</u>cast

   (A) similar to
   (B) earlier
   (C) remove from
   (D) related to

3. <u>co</u>author   <u>co</u>operate

   (A) before
   (B) after
   (C) again
   (D) together

4. descend<u>ant</u>   inhabit<u>ant</u>

   (A) one who
   (B) worthy of
   (C) act of
   (D) against

5. content<u>ment</u>   engage<u>ment</u>

   (A) opposite
   (B) lacking
   (C) state of being
   (D) formerly

Directions: Read the sentence and the question. Choose the word that best answers the question.

6. Mr. Cashman owns an _____ car. Which word would suggest that the car is very old?

   (A) authentic   (C) antique
   (B) inexpensive   (D) imported

7. When the storm hit, the lost hiker found _____ in an abandoned hunting lodge. Which word would suggest that the hiker found protection?

   (A) shelter   (C) hospitality
   (B) success   (D) assistance

Directions: Read the meaning of the original word. Then choose the modern word that comes from the original word.

8. Which word probably comes from the Latin word *specere,* meaning "to see"?

   (A) speck   (C) spacecraft
   (B) spectator   (D) speechless

9. Which word probably comes from the Middle English word *launde,* meaning "grass-covered area"?

   (A) laundry   (C) lane
   (B) lumber   (D) lawn

Stop

Language Arts

PRACTICE 8 • Sentences

SAMPLES

Directions: Choose the simple subject of the sentence.

    A. The <u>rear</u> <u>tire</u> <u>fell</u> off my <u>bike</u>.
        Ⓐ   Ⓑ Ⓒ   Ⓓ

Directions: Choose the simple predicate.

    B. <u>Colin's</u> <u>sister</u> <u>lost</u> his <u>notebook</u>.
        Ⓐ   Ⓑ   Ⓒ   Ⓓ

Directions: Find the answer that is a complete sentence written correctly.

    C. Ⓐ   See many stars on a winter night.
        Ⓑ   She brought a telescope they set it up on the porch.
        Ⓒ   Sirius, the brightest star in the sky.
        Ⓓ   Orion's belt is made up of three bright stars.

> **Tips and Reminders**
>
> - To find the subject of a sentence, ask yourself *who* or *what* is doing or did something ("The <u>tire</u> fell . . .").
>
> - To find the predicate of a sentence, ask yourself *what* the person or thing is doing or did ("Colin's sister <u>lost</u> . . .").
>
> - A complete sentence has a subject and a verb and expresses a complete thought. Watch out for answers that include two sentences run together.

PRACTICE

Directions: Choose the simple subject of the sentence.

    1. <u>Todd's</u> <u>mother</u> <u>works</u> at the <u>bank</u>.
        Ⓐ   Ⓑ   Ⓒ   Ⓓ

    2. The <u>jet</u> <u>plane</u> <u>left</u> a white <u>trail</u> in the sky.
        Ⓐ Ⓑ   Ⓒ   Ⓓ

    3. <u>Students</u> at our <u>school</u> are <u>encouraged</u> to play <u>sports</u>.
        Ⓐ   Ⓑ   Ⓒ   Ⓓ

Go On →

PRACTICE 8 • Sentences (continued)

Directions: Choose the simple predicate of the sentence.

4. Jackals live in family groups, not packs.
   Ⓐ   Ⓑ   Ⓒ   Ⓓ

5. Two young brothers rescued an injured mountain climber.
        Ⓐ   Ⓑ   Ⓒ   Ⓓ

6. Gene and his sister entered the talent show.
   Ⓐ   Ⓑ   Ⓒ   Ⓓ

Directions: Find the answer that is a complete sentence written correctly.

7. Ⓐ Very beautiful this time of year.
   Ⓑ The leaves turn different colors.
   Ⓒ People taking photos of trees.
   Ⓓ The leaves fall to the ground winter soon follows.

8. Ⓐ Kevin has started a new hobby.
   Ⓑ He is learning photography he is taking many pictures.
   Ⓒ Developing his own photos.
   Ⓓ Photographs as gifts to his friends.

9. Ⓐ Shorter days and longer nights.
   Ⓑ A flock of geese honking.
   Ⓒ Flying overhead in a V-pattern.
   Ⓓ The geese are heading south for the winter.

10. Ⓐ Traveling at 22,000 miles an hour.
    Ⓑ Space is becoming cluttered with junk the junk can be dangerous.
    Ⓒ Dead satellites, nuts, bolts, and bits of wire orbit the earth.
    Ⓓ Present a threat to astronauts.

11. Ⓐ Bogs are not what they seem on the surface.
    Ⓑ Formed in ponds or lakes where deep water stands still.
    Ⓒ Plants growing at the water's edge.
    Ⓓ Dangerous to walk on a bog.

12. Ⓐ Learned all about animal tracking.
    Ⓑ Students studying animal tracks.
    Ⓒ The students found fox tracks the tracks showed distinct claw marks.
    Ⓓ They could tell by the fox's tracks that it had been running.

13. Ⓐ Decided to try winter camping.
    Ⓑ Temperatures dropped below zero during the night.
    Ⓒ Didn't dress warmly enough.
    Ⓓ The boys packed up their things they couldn't wait to get home.

14. Ⓐ Shelly at a craft show.
    Ⓑ Many exhibits under a large tent.
    Ⓒ Shelly bought a candle and some earrings.
    Ⓓ Didn't have enough money to buy a tie-dyed shirt.

Stop

Mathematics

PRACTICE 9 • Number Operations

Directions: Choose the best answer to each question.

SAMPLES

A. What number belongs in the box to make this number sentence true?

$$7 \times (2 + 6) = (2 + 6) \times \square$$

- Ⓐ 56
- Ⓑ 42
- Ⓒ 13
- Ⓓ 7

B. If $22 - n > 18$, then

- Ⓐ $n > 4$
- Ⓒ $n < 4$
- Ⓑ $n = 3$
- Ⓓ $n = 4$

C. Which point is located at $(3, 4)$?

- Ⓐ F
- Ⓑ G
- Ⓒ H
- Ⓓ J

Tips and Reminders

- Read each number sentence carefully. Try each answer choice in the number sentence until you find the one that is correct.

- In an ordered pair, find the first number by counting to the right. The second number tells how many spaces to count up.

PRACTICE

1. What number belongs in the box to make this number sentence true?

$$34 \times \square = 1$$

- Ⓐ ⁻34
- Ⓒ ⁻1
- Ⓑ $\frac{1}{34}$
- Ⓓ 0

2. If $56 \div n = 8$, then $n =$

- Ⓐ 64
- Ⓑ 48
- Ⓒ 7
- Ⓓ 6

Go On

3. What coordinates are shown by the point on the grid?

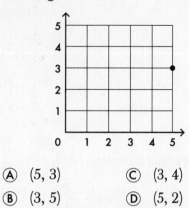

Ⓐ (5, 3)   Ⓒ (3, 4)

Ⓑ (3, 5)   Ⓓ (5, 2)

4. Which equation represents the statement, "The sum of 17 and b is 40"?

Ⓐ $b + 40 = 17$

Ⓑ $17 + 40 = b$

Ⓒ $17 - b = 40$

Ⓓ $17 + b = 40$

5. What number belongs in the box to make the number sentence true?

$6 \times 5 = 36 - \square$

Ⓐ 30   Ⓒ 6

Ⓑ 11   Ⓓ 5

6. What is another way to write 4×7?

Ⓐ $7 \times 7 \times 7 \times 7$

Ⓑ $7 + 7 + 7 + 7$

Ⓒ $(4 + 7) \times 4$

Ⓓ $(4 + 4 + 4 + 4) \times 7$

7. If $5 \times n > 20$, then

Ⓐ $n = 4$ Ⓒ $n < 4$

Ⓑ $n > 4$ Ⓓ $n = 5$

8. If $48 + n < 65$, then

Ⓐ $n = 17$ Ⓒ $n = 113$

Ⓑ $n > 17$ Ⓓ $n < 17$

9. What number belongs in the box to make this number sentence true?

$\square \div 6 = 7$

Ⓐ 1   Ⓒ 42

Ⓑ 13   Ⓓ 49

10. What is another way to write 5×8?

Ⓐ $(5 \times 3) \times 8$

Ⓑ $(2 + 3) \times (3 + 5)$

Ⓒ $(8 \times 8) + 5$

Ⓓ $(8 + 5) \times 8$

11. Which equation represents the statement, "The product of 2 and c is 10"?

Ⓐ $10 - c = 2$

Ⓑ $2 + 10 = c$

Ⓒ $2 \times c = 10$

Ⓓ $2 + c = 10$

12. Which point is located at $(1, 4)$?

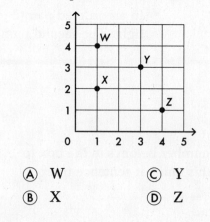

Ⓐ W   Ⓒ Y

Ⓑ X   Ⓓ Z

Stop

Reading

PRACTICE 10 • Interpreting Text

Directions: Read each passage. Then answer the questions that follow.

SAMPLES

Everything had gone well at dinner. Martin's children had been little darlings. His boss had seemed to enjoy the meal he had prepared. Now, with his boss gone and the children safely tucked into bed, he could take it easy.

Martin took off his shoes and collapsed into a comfortable chair, relieved to be able to let his hair down at last. Then he glanced into the mirror on the wall and gasped. Martin was mortified to discover that a piece of spinach had been lodged between his front teeth all evening. He felt as if all his efforts to impress his boss had just gone down the drain.

A. To "let his hair down" means to —

- (A) relax
- (B) grow his hair long
- (C) change his hair style
- (D) speak freely

B. In the second paragraph, the word <u>mortified</u> means —

- (A) pleased
- (B) delighted
- (C) exhausted
- (D) embarrassed

C. His efforts had "gone down the drain" means that they were —

- (A) lost in the sink
- (B) wasted
- (C) covered with spinach
- (D) rinsed off

Tips and Reminders

- For words you don't know, look in the passage for clues that can help you guess their meaning.

- If a sentence doesn't seem to make sense the way it is written, look for a "hidden" or implied meaning. Use context clues to help figure out what the sentence really means.

Go On

PRACTICE

> For many years Anna had heard about old Uncle Jasper, whose tightfisted ways had earned him a great deal of criticism. Among members of the family, he was about as welcome as the flu. But finally, Anna was going to meet this man she had heard so much about.
>
> Anna was usually quiet and reserved when meeting strangers, but when she saw Uncle Jasper, she boldly asked him how he got to be such a miser. Somehow, Uncle Jasper thought she asked him how he got to be such a wise man. He told her that wisdom comes from age and experience. "And that's straight from the horse's mouth," he added.
>
> While Anna was perplexed by his answer, her parents were relieved. Of course, from that point on, Uncle Jasper thought Anna was the cat's meow.

1. In the second paragraph, the word <u>miser</u> means –

   Ⓐ a popular person

   Ⓑ a thoughtful person

   Ⓒ a stingy person

   Ⓓ an unmarried man

2. In the third paragraph, the word <u>perplexed</u> means –

   Ⓐ pleased

   Ⓑ satisfied

   Ⓒ concerned

   Ⓓ puzzled

3. The phrase "straight from the horse's mouth" means –

   Ⓐ spoken by a horse

   Ⓑ from a trustworthy source

   Ⓒ eaten by a horse

   Ⓓ with a sense of pride

4. Uncle Jasper thought that Anna was "the cat's meow" means that he thought she –

   Ⓐ was special

   Ⓑ looked like a cat

   Ⓒ purred too much

   Ⓓ had whiskers

Go On

Sue set a record on the auction block. Sue, who is not a person but a group of bones, is perhaps the most impressive dinosaur fossil discovered to date. Estimated to be 85 million years old, the fossil sold for 8.4 million dollars. The fossil generated big bucks because it is the most complete *Tyrannosaurus rex* skeleton ever found. The skeleton was purchased by a Chicago museum, aided by several corporate sponsors. Some of these large companies helped to foot the bill in hopes of getting replicas of the fossil. These replicas will be displayed at a theme park and in traveling exhibits. The original fossil will be on display at the museum.

Sue, named for its discoverer Susan Hendrickson, includes about 400 bones. The skull alone is five feet long. The entire fossil will be about 50 feet long when it is reassembled.

5. The fossil "generated big bucks" means that it —

Ⓐ gave birth to large deer

Ⓑ had large bones

Ⓒ earned a lot of money

Ⓓ found many large teeth

6. The phrase "foot the bill" means to —

Ⓐ pay for

Ⓑ find footprints

Ⓒ step on the beak

Ⓓ kick the bones

7. In the first paragraph, the word <u>corporate</u> means —

Ⓐ military

Ⓑ business

Ⓒ bodily

Ⓓ advertising

8. In the first paragraph, the word <u>replicas</u> means —

Ⓐ copies

Ⓑ autographs

Ⓒ earnings

Ⓓ offspring

Stop

Language Arts

PRACTICE 11 • Punctuation

Directions: Choose the sentence that is written with correct punctuation.

SAMPLES

A.   Ⓐ Dr Carter has an office on Main Street.

     Ⓑ She has two chairs, an x-ray room, and a waiting room.

     Ⓒ She is the only dentist in Farwell West Virginia.

     Ⓓ Its great that she has so many clients.

B.   Ⓐ Some kids think they invented certain fashions?

     Ⓑ They dont' know that their parents wore bell-bottoms.

     Ⓒ "You must be kidding, Josh said.

     Ⓓ He thought the style was new.

> **Tips and Reminders**
>
> • Check every punctuation mark. Decide if the mark is needed, and make sure it is the right kind of punctuation.
>
> • Read the sentence to yourself to decide if it sounds right. If there is a pause in the sentence, there should be a punctuation mark.

PRACTICE

1.   Ⓐ Is there a party at Teresas' house?

     Ⓑ It's going to be on Friday.

     Ⓒ She lives on Elm St, near the bank.

     Ⓓ Please bring these things, a snack, a video, and a game.

2.   Ⓐ Sometimes stores raise their prices.

     Ⓑ They lower the prices: claiming to have a great sale.

     Ⓒ Judy said "I don't believe it!"

     Ⓓ Im afraid it's true?

3. Ⓐ The largest pumpkin, ever grown, weighed half a ton.

Ⓑ Sometimes pumpkins grow; so fast that they explode!

Ⓒ The wall of a giant pumpkin may be a foot thick.

Ⓓ Pumpkins may grow, 10 inches a day.

4. Ⓐ Kenny's family is moving to Evanston Illinois.

Ⓑ His mother got a job with General Bicycle Co.

Ⓒ He's going to start school there in January 1999.

Ⓓ "I'll miss you all he said.

5. Ⓐ "Andrew, can you name the state capital?" asked Molly.

Ⓑ Sure, it's Augusta, Portland, or Freeport" he guessed.

Ⓒ "Yes, but which one," Molly asked.

Ⓓ "Thats a good question, he said.

6. Ⓐ Pablo Picasso was born in Malaga, Spain.

Ⓑ We went to see a Picasso exhibit but, it was closed.

Ⓒ It had paintings from his Blue, Rose, and, classical periods.

Ⓓ Well I think he was great!

7. Ⓐ My aunt lives in Big Sur California.

Ⓑ She makes honey that is flavored with sage?

Ⓒ I didnt know there were different flavors of honey.

Ⓓ This jar is labeled August 24, 1997.

8. Ⓐ I read all kinds of stories, poems, and, books.

Ⓑ "The Lottery" is a short story by Shirley Jackson.

Ⓒ Its my favorite short story.

Ⓓ Marias favorite story is The Lady or the Tiger?

9. Ⓐ "Where have you been" asked Mr. Ames?

Ⓑ "I had to stop at the store on my way to work, said Clint."

Ⓒ "You are supposed to be here by nine," said Mr. Ames.

Ⓓ "Yes I'm sorry," Clint replied.

10. Ⓐ Leonardo da Vinci was a great inventor, and he was an artist.

Ⓑ The *Mona Lisa* a famous painting, hangs in the Louvre.

Ⓒ He drew sketches of airplanes but he never built one.

Ⓓ He lived mainly in Florence Italy.

Stop

Mathematics

PRACTICE 12 • Geometry

Directions: Choose the best answer to each question.

SAMPLES

A. Which of these is an obtuse angle?

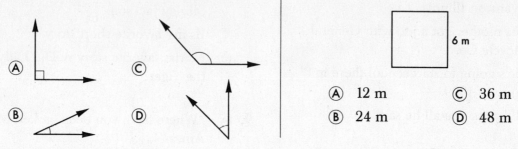

(A)

(B)

(C)

(D)

B. What is the perimeter of this square?

6 m

(A) 12 m   (C) 36 m

(B) 24 m   (D) 48 m

Tips and Reminders

• Look at the pictures for information. Draw your own picture if it will help you answer the question.

• After choosing an answer, read the question again to make sure you have answered it correctly.

PRACTICE

1. What is the diameter of this circular pool?

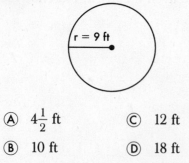

r = 9 ft

(A) $4\frac{1}{2}$ ft   (C) 12 ft

(B) 10 ft   (D) 18 ft

2. What is the volume of this rectangular prism?

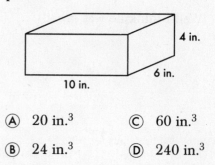

4 in.

6 in.

10 in.

(A) 20 in.³   (C) 60 in.³

(B) 24 in.³   (D) 240 in.³

3. Which figure has a triangular face?

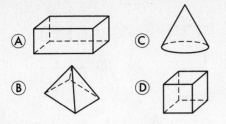

Ⓐ Ⓒ Ⓑ Ⓓ

4. Which of these is an acute angle?

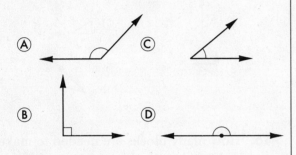

Ⓐ Ⓒ Ⓑ Ⓓ

5. What is the radius of a circle with a diameter of 20 cm?

Ⓐ 5 cm Ⓒ 40 cm
Ⓑ 10 cm Ⓓ 62.8 cm

6. What is the area of a rectangular wall that measures 8 ft by 12 ft?

Ⓐ 20 ft² Ⓒ 80 ft²
Ⓑ 72 ft² Ⓓ 96 ft²

7. Which angle measures 90°?

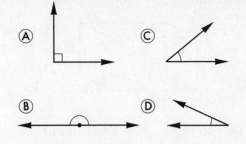

Ⓐ Ⓒ Ⓑ Ⓓ

8. What shape is the face of a cube?

Ⓐ square Ⓒ cylinder
Ⓑ triangle Ⓓ sphere

9. What is the volume of this rectangular prism?

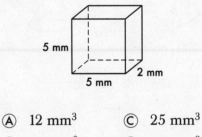

5 mm

5 mm 2 mm

Ⓐ 12 mm³ Ⓒ 25 mm³
Ⓑ 20 mm³ Ⓓ 50 mm³

10. A rectangular garden measures 12 ft by 20 ft. What is the perimeter of the garden?

Ⓐ 32 ft Ⓒ 120 ft
Ⓑ 64 ft Ⓓ 240 ft

11. What is the volume of this rectangular fish tank?

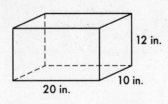

12 in.

10 in.

20 in.

(A) 42 in.³
(C) 240 in.³
(B) 120 in.³
(D) 2400 in.³

12. Which figure has exactly 6 faces?

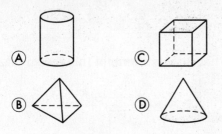

(A)

(C)

(B)

(D)

13. What is the radius of this circle?

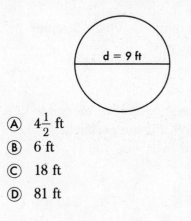

d = 9 ft

(A) $4\frac{1}{2}$ ft
(B) 6 ft
(C) 18 ft
(D) 81 ft

14. Which figure shows a rotation of 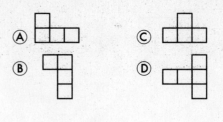 ?

(A)

(C)

(B)

(D)

15. Which figure shows a reflection of ?

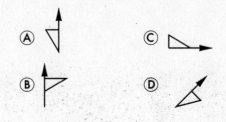

(A)

(C)

(B)

(D)

16. How many blocks are needed to make this figure?

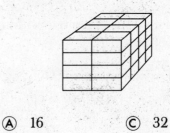

(A) 16
(C) 32
(B) 24
(D) 64

Stop

Reading

PRACTICE 13 • Main Idea and Details

SAMPLES

Directions: Read this passage. Then answer the questions below.

Marco's plane was landing. Jamie's family was ready for his visit, although Jamie wished he knew more Italian than simply *benvenuto*, which means "welcome." The boys had exchanged a couple of letters, but those hadn't revealed much beyond where Marco lived. Jamie was afraid that he and Marco would have nothing in common and wouldn't be able to communicate.

As Marco walked into the airport terminal, he greeted Jamie warmly. Noticing the cap Jamie wore, Marco exclaimed, "Ah, the New York Yankees. These are my favorite! I watch them on TV."

A. Which is the best title for this passage?

   Ⓐ "The New York Yankees"

   Ⓑ "A Bumpy Landing"

   Ⓒ "Waiting for Marco's Arrival"

   Ⓓ "*Benvenuto* Means Welcome"

B. Which detail shows how Marco knew which team was Jamie's favorite?

   Ⓐ Marco met Jamie in New York.

   Ⓑ Marco saw the hat Jamie was wearing.

   Ⓒ Jamie had written about the Yankees in a letter.

   Ⓓ Jamie was watching the Yankees on TV.

Tips and Reminders

- Scan the questions quickly to see what you should look for in the passage.

- To find the main idea or topic of a passage or paragraph, decide what the whole passage or paragraph is mostly about. To find supporting details, look back at the passage.

- Try to answer each question before looking at the answer choices.

Go On

PRACTICE

Directions: Read this passage about emergency readiness. Then answer questions 1–6 on the next page.

Are you prepared for an emergency? Too few people are as prepared as they should be, but there are some simple precautions you can take. It doesn't matter if the area where you live is prone to hurricanes, tornadoes, earthquakes, mudslides, blizzards, or some other natural disaster. Most of these tips can be applied anywhere.

Often in an emergency, electric power goes out. Flashlights are always safer than candles as a substitute for electric light. Be sure that you store a couple of flashlights where you can locate them in the dark. Check the batteries every few months. Most TVs are useless when the power goes out, so you can't turn on the TV to get information. A portable radio is essential as a means of keeping informed in an emergency. Like flashlight batteries, radio batteries should be checked occasionally. Keep some spares on hand. It's also helpful to know which radio station provides emergency information in your area.

It's a good idea to shut off electrical equipment and gas lines. This action can help prevent blown fuses, gas leaks, and other problems.

If you have well water where you live, the well won't pump if the power goes out. Even if you have a public water supply, it's a good idea to be prepared by storing several unopened gallons of drinking water.

Do not use a gas oven for heat, even in an emergency. If possible, keep a supply of extra blankets, rain gear, and boots to help you stay warm and dry.

With family members, plan a place to meet if you are separated or unable to get to your home in an emergency. You might arrange to get in touch with one particular relative, for example. Another possibility is meeting at an emergency shelter. Many communities set up these shelters in wide-scale disasters. Their locations are reported on local radio stations.

While you can't prevent natural disasters, preparation can make them far easier to endure.

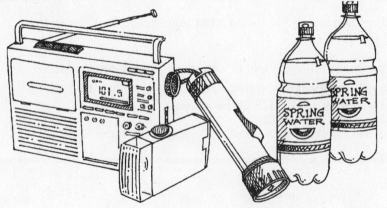

Go On

1. Which title best fits this passage?

Ⓐ "Avoiding Tornadoes"

Ⓑ "Staying Dry in the Mud"

Ⓒ "Why You Need New Batteries"

Ⓓ "Simple Steps to Emergency Readiness"

2. According to this passage, which is the most common source of problems during a natural disaster?

Ⓐ mud

Ⓑ flooding

Ⓒ power failure

Ⓓ cold weather

3. What is the main idea of the first paragraph?

Ⓐ It doesn't matter where you live.

Ⓑ A blizzard can be a natural disaster.

Ⓒ Too few people are prepared for emergencies.

Ⓓ Some areas do not have earthquakes or mudslides.

4. What is the main topic of this passage?

Ⓐ preparing for natural disasters

Ⓑ hurricanes and tornadoes

Ⓒ buying flashlights and batteries

Ⓓ emergency shelters

5. Which detail supports the idea that a portable radio would be useful during a natural disaster?

Ⓐ You should shut off gas lines during an emergency.

Ⓑ Radio batteries should be checked occasionally.

Ⓒ Be sure to have a few spare batteries on hand.

Ⓓ Some radio stations broadcast emergency information.

6. How can family members help protect one another in an emergency?

Ⓐ Make sure they have access to a public water supply.

Ⓑ Arrange a place to meet in case they are separated.

Ⓒ Find out if their area has earthquakes.

Ⓓ Try to prevent natural disasters.

Go On

Directions: Read this passage about sumo wrestling. Then answer questions 7–10.

Sumo wrestling has long been a favorite spectator sport in Japan. Although it became popular in the 1600s, sumo actually began about 2000 years ago.

A sumo match starts with a number of ancient rituals. First, the wrestlers clap their hands to awaken the gods. Next, they throw salt on the ground to cleanse it. Finally, they stamp on the ground to drive out evil. Then the match begins. The wrestlers enter the ring and crouch down, placing their hands on the ground. At the referee's signal they charge, trying to throw their opponent to the ground or out of the ring, which is 12 feet in diameter.

A wrestler's weight gives him a low center of gravity. This makes it harder for his opponent to throw or trip him. For this reason many sumo wrestlers weigh more than 350 pounds! The wrestlers eat many meals a day to gain weight— traditionally, meals of rice, tofu, and vegetables. Recently, sumo wrestlers have also begun to eat meat, which adds weight more rapidly.

7. What is this passage mostly about?

  Ⓐ the sport of sumo wrestling

  Ⓑ how wrestlers prepare for a match

  Ⓒ the history of wrestling

  Ⓓ eating healthful food

8. Which detail supports the idea that sumo is a very old sport?

  Ⓐ Matches begin with ancient rituals.

  Ⓑ Sumo wrestlers are very heavy.

  Ⓒ A wrestler has a low center of gravity.

  Ⓓ Sumo is popular in Japan.

9. Which detail explains why many sumo wrestlers weigh more than 350 pounds?

  Ⓐ The wrestlers crouch down.

  Ⓑ Wrestlers eat rice and tofu.

  Ⓒ Wrestlers must wake up sleeping gods.

  Ⓓ The wrestler's weight makes him difficult to move.

10. Which title best fits this passage?

  Ⓐ "Gaining Weight"

  Ⓑ "An Ancient Sport"

  Ⓒ "The Center of Gravity"

  Ⓓ "Good vs. Evil"

Stop

Language Arts

PRACTICE 14 • Capitalization

Directions: Read the passage and look at the underlined parts. If the underlined part has a mistake in capitalization, choose the answer that shows correct capitalization. If the underlined part is correct, choose answer D, "Correct as it is."

SAMPLES

> I. M. Pei, a famous architect, designed a pyramid in front of a
> (A)   museum in <u>Paris, france</u>. Frank Lloyd Wright was also very well known
> (B)   for his designs. He designed the <u>Guggenheim Museum</u> in New York.

A.
- Ⓐ paris, france
- Ⓑ Paris, France
- Ⓒ paris, France
- Ⓓ Correct as it is

B.
- Ⓐ Guggenheim museum
- Ⓑ guggenheim museum
- Ⓒ guggenheim Museum
- Ⓓ Correct as it is

 **Tips and Reminders**

- Check every word that has a capital letter. Decide if the word should be capitalized or not.
- Watch for words that are not capitalized but should be.

PRACTICE

> (1)   Would you like to visit the <u>Middle east</u>? Many Muslims who live
> (2)   there celebrate the <u>holiday of ramadan</u> for a month. People don't eat
> from sunrise to sundown.

1.
- Ⓐ middle east
- Ⓑ Middle East
- Ⓒ middle East
- Ⓓ Correct as it is

2.
- Ⓐ Holiday of Ramadan
- Ⓑ Holiday of ramadan
- Ⓒ holiday of Ramadan
- Ⓓ Correct as it is

Go On →

(3)   603 Candlestick lane
(4)   Toledo, Ohio
December 20, 1998

(5)   Dear tammy,
        You wouldn't believe what happened in school today. We had a
(6)   magician at our assembly. The magician made the principal, dr. Rowe,
disappear! He did come back, though. He stepped out of a cloud of
(7)   smoke and said, "i'm ba-a-ack!"
(8)   I have to go now. I need to memorize a poem, "A hillside thaw,"
(9)   for school. write back soon.

(10)   Your friend,
Tracey

3. Ⓐ 603 candlestick Lane
Ⓑ 603 Candlestick Lane
Ⓒ 603 candlestick lane
Ⓓ Correct as it is

4. Ⓐ toledo, Ohio
Ⓑ Toledo, ohio
Ⓒ toledo, ohio
Ⓓ Correct as it is

5. Ⓐ Dear Tammy
Ⓑ dear tammy
Ⓒ dear Tammy
Ⓓ Correct as it is

6. Ⓐ principal, Dr. rowe
Ⓑ Principal, dr. Rowe
Ⓒ principal, Dr. Rowe
Ⓓ Correct as it is

7. Ⓐ said, "I'm
Ⓑ Said, "I'm
Ⓒ Said, "i'm
Ⓓ Correct as it is

8. Ⓐ A Hillside Thaw
Ⓑ a Hillside Thaw
Ⓒ A hillside Thaw
Ⓓ Correct as it is

9. Ⓐ Write Back Soon.
Ⓑ Write back soon.
Ⓒ write back Soon.
Ⓓ Correct as it is

10. Ⓐ Your Friend
Ⓑ your friend
Ⓒ your Friend
Ⓓ Correct as it is

Stop

Mathematics

PRACTICE 15 • Measurement

Directions: Choose the best answer to each question.

SAMPLES

A. Dennis napped from 4:15 until 5:45. How long did he nap?

- Ⓐ 30 min
- Ⓑ 45 min
- Ⓒ 1 hr 30 min
- Ⓓ 1 hr 45 min

B. Which unit is most appropriate for measuring the amount of water in a full bathtub?

- Ⓐ gallons
- Ⓑ cups
- Ⓒ pounds
- Ⓓ ounces

> **Tips and Reminders**
> - Underline or jot down important information to help you answer each question.
> - Draw your own picture if it will help you answer the question.
> - Make an estimate. Check to see if any of the answer choices is close to your estimate.
> - Try each answer choice given. Rule out those that make no sense.

PRACTICE

1. Troy walked 5.5 kilometers. How many meters did he walk?

- Ⓐ 0.55 m
- Ⓒ 550 m
- Ⓑ 50.5 m
- Ⓓ 5500 m

2. The length of a gym is 150 feet. How many yards is that?

- Ⓐ 5 yd
- Ⓒ 50 yd
- Ⓑ 30 yd
- Ⓓ 75 yd

3. Lena made 2 quarts of lemonade. She drank 1 cup. How many cups of lemonade did she have left?

- Ⓐ 3 cups
- Ⓒ 6 cups
- Ⓑ 5 cups
- Ⓓ 7 cups

4. Biff put 3200 milliliters of oil into an engine. How many liters is that?

- Ⓐ 0.32 L
- Ⓒ 32 L
- Ⓑ 3.2 L
- Ⓓ 320 L

Go On

Use the map below and an inch ruler to answer questions 5–6.

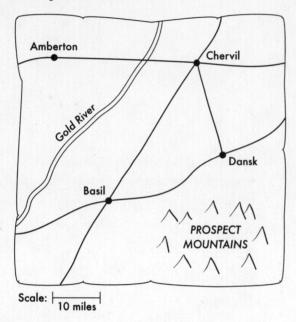

Scale: |———————| 10 miles

5. About how far is it by road from Basil to Chervil?

  Ⓐ 15 miles   Ⓒ 35 miles

  Ⓑ 25 miles   Ⓓ 45 miles

6. Milo drove from Amberton to Chervil to Dansk. About how many miles did he drive in all?

  Ⓐ 20 miles   Ⓒ 40 miles

  Ⓑ 30 miles   Ⓓ 50 miles

7. The sixth grade held a car wash on Saturday morning from 7:30 to 11:00. How long did the car wash last?

  Ⓐ 7 hr

  Ⓑ 4 hr 30 min

  Ⓒ 4 hr

  Ⓓ 3 hr 30 min

8. A school assembly began at 9:45 and lasted 1 hour 20 minutes. What time did it end?

  Ⓐ 11:15

  Ⓑ 11:05

  Ⓒ 10:20

  Ⓓ 10:05

9. About how much liquid does a teacup hold?

  Ⓐ 6 ounces

  Ⓑ 6 pints

  Ⓒ 6 quarts

  Ⓓ 6 gallons

10. Donna's construction company owns a 2-ton truck. How many pounds are there in 2 tons?

  Ⓐ 1400 lb

  Ⓑ 2000 lb

  Ⓒ 4000 lb

  Ⓓ 20,000 lb

Go On →

PRACTICE 15 • Measurement (continued)

11. Look at the map of the mall shown below. What is the distance through the hallway from the door of the shoe store to the door of the sporting goods store? (Use a centimeter ruler.)

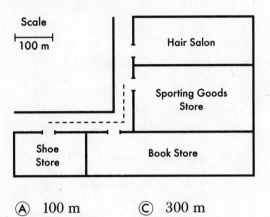

Ⓐ 100 m   Ⓒ 300 m

Ⓑ 200 m   Ⓓ 400 m

12. A spaghetti dinner begins at 6:30 P.M. and will last $1\frac{1}{2}$ hours. At what time will it end?

Ⓐ 7:00 P.M.

Ⓑ 7:30 P.M.

Ⓒ 7:45 P.M.

Ⓓ 8:00 P.M.

13. Which unit is most appropriate for measuring the mass of a bluebird?

Ⓐ grams

Ⓑ milligrams

Ⓒ pounds

Ⓓ kilograms

14. The height of Jody's bedroom ceiling is 96 inches. How many feet is 96 inches?

Ⓐ 7 ft   Ⓒ 9 ft 6 in.

Ⓑ 8 ft   Ⓓ 10 ft

15. About how tall is the back of a school chair?

Ⓐ 13 in.   Ⓒ 30 ft

Ⓑ 3 ft   Ⓓ 130 in.

16. Which is the most appropriate unit for measuring the length of a river?

Ⓐ inches

Ⓑ feet

Ⓒ yards

Ⓓ miles

17. Which is the most likely temperature for a snowy winter day?

Ⓐ 20°F

Ⓑ 40°F

Ⓒ 60°F

Ⓓ 80°F

18. About how long is a pick-up truck?

Ⓐ 4 m

Ⓑ 8 m

Ⓒ 12 m

Ⓓ 20 m

53

Stop

Reading

PRACTICE 16 • Text Structure

SAMPLES

Directions: Read this passage about sunflowers. Then answer the questions below.

Sunflower designs seem to be everywhere: on hats and clothing, on posters, on plates and coffee mugs. Although the designs usually show large, perky flowers with black centers and cheerful yellow petals, Nature is more creative. Real-life sunflowers come not only in yellow but also in shades of white, red, brown, and orange. Sunflower blossoms may range in size from only an inch wide to more than a foot across.

Sunflowers are easy to plant. Just press seeds a couple of inches into garden soil. With plenty of sun and occasional watering, they are almost guaranteed to bloom. When they do, you can pick the flowers or leave them in place. After the flowers fade, you can even eat the dried seeds—if you collect them before the birds do. Birds love sunflower seeds, and they can certainly tell the difference between a sunflower design and the real thing!

A. According to this passage, what should you do after the sunflowers fade?

Ⓐ pick the flowers

Ⓑ press the seeds into the soil

Ⓒ eat the dried seeds

Ⓓ give the plants plenty of sun

B. If you want to save the seeds, you have to collect them as soon as they are ready because –

Ⓐ the seeds will rot

Ⓑ they will change colors

Ⓒ the seeds will blow away

Ⓓ birds will eat them

C. How do real sunflowers differ from sunflower designs?

Ⓐ They are yellow.

Ⓑ They are more varied.

Ⓒ They are less colorful.

Ⓓ They are smaller.

Tips and Reminders

• Look for signal words in the passage to help find the sequence of events, causes and effects, or comparisons and contrasts.

• Read the passage carefully. Events may not be described in the order in which they occur.

Go On

PRACTICE

Directions: Read this passage about a problem in Indonesia. Then answer questions 1–4.

People often rely on predictable cycles of nature, but sometimes Nature plays tricks. In Indonesia, a group of more than 17,000 islands in Southeast Asia, many people rely on agriculture to feed themselves and make a living. Once a year, farmers and logging companies set fires to burn fields and forests to clear land for planting. They rely on annual rains, called monsoons, to put out the fires. However, in 1997, El Niño, a warm ocean current, changed the weather patterns, and the usual monsoons were delayed for several months. As a result, massive clouds of smoke settled like a blanket over much of Indonesia and neighboring Malaysia. Thousands of people experienced breathing difficulties. The smoke also hindered visibility and was blamed for causing a large plane crash and collisions between ships.

At one point more than 40,000 people were called in to fight the smoky fires. Strong winds also helped to clear the smoke. Still, in an effort to control the source of the smoke, the government revoked the licenses of several logging companies.

1. Farmers and loggers in Indonesia set fires in order to –

Ⓐ avoid the monsoons

Ⓑ raise the price of crops

Ⓒ clear land for planting

Ⓓ complain about the government

2. Which of these events occurred last?

Ⓐ Loggers set fires to forests.

Ⓑ Loggers lost their licenses.

Ⓒ Monsoons put out the fires.

Ⓓ The monsoons were delayed.

3. In 1997, how was the weather in Indonesia different from usual?

Ⓐ The rains came later.

Ⓑ The rains were heavier.

Ⓒ The winds were stronger.

Ⓓ The temperature was warmer.

4. The clouds of smoke over Indonesia began to clear because of –

Ⓐ a large plane crash

Ⓑ the effects of El Niño

Ⓒ collisions between ships

Ⓓ strong winds

Go On

Directions: Read this passage about a man who lives in Minnesota. Then answer questions 5–10 on the next page.

My father once told me how he came to live in Minnesota. He had a job laying railroad track in Mississippi. It was hard work, but the worst part was the mosquitoes. They were as big as blackbirds! At dusk, great swarms of them came out to feed. To avoid the mosquitoes, the workers always tried to make sure they were home before sundown.

One day Dad had to work late. He worked as fast as he could, but soon the sun began to set and a huge swarm of mosquitoes came looking for blood. Dad grabbed his tools and ran. The only place to hide was in an old locomotive boiler lying along the track. He jumped inside and slammed the hatch. The boiler was made of steel, so he figured he'd be safe until morning.

But the mosquitoes drilled right through the steel with their blood-sucking "snouts," as Dad called them. Each time a snout bored through, Dad clinched it on the inside with his claw hammer so the mosquito could not get away. When he had several dozen clinched to the boiler, he began to feel a gentle rocking motion. The mosquitoes were flying away and taking the boiler with them!

After a few hours, Dad took the hammer and started releasing the snouts. Each time a freed mosquito flew off, the boiler sank lower. With a little luck and good timing, Dad managed a perfect landing in a wheat field. When all the mosquitoes had left, he emerged from the boiler and looked around. The place where he had landed turned out to be Minnesota. It had more hills and cooler temperatures than Mississippi, but it looked like a nice place, and so he stayed on. I think the mosquitoes stayed on, too.

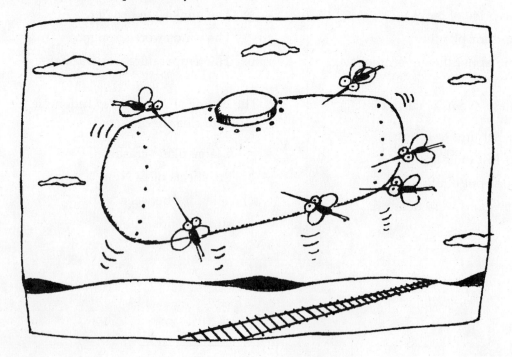

5. Which event involving the narrator's father happened first?

   Ⓐ He hid inside a boiler.

   Ⓑ He grabbed his tools and ran.

   Ⓒ He emerged from the boiler.

   Ⓓ He worked in Mississippi.

6. The railroad workers always went home before sundown in order to –

   Ⓐ avoid the mosquitoes

   Ⓑ have dinner on time

   Ⓒ get plenty of rest

   Ⓓ avoid making mistakes in the dark

7. How was the narrator's father different from the other railroad workers?

   Ⓐ He did not like Mississippi.

   Ⓑ He had to work late.

   Ⓒ He was not afraid of mosquitoes.

   Ⓓ He was a pilot.

8. What happened after Dad began releasing the mosquitoes' snouts?

   Ⓐ The mosquitoes bit him.

   Ⓑ Dad hid in the boiler.

   Ⓒ The boiler sank lower.

   Ⓓ Dad felt a gentle rocking motion.

9. Why did Dad stay on in Minnesota?

   Ⓐ There were no mosquitoes there.

   Ⓑ He wanted to grow wheat.

   Ⓒ It looked like a nice place.

   Ⓓ His son lived in Minnesota.

10. According to this passage, how is Minnesota different from Mississippi?

    Ⓐ It has no mosquitoes.

    Ⓑ It has no railroads.

    Ⓒ It has more blackbirds.

    Ⓓ It has cooler temperatures.

Stop

PRACTICE 17 • Spelling

Directions: Read each sentence. If one of the underlined words is misspelled, fill in the bubble under that word. If all of the words are spelled correctly, fill in the bubble under answer D, "No mistake."

SAMPLES

A. That <u>willow</u> tree has <u>groan</u> two <u>meters</u> taller. <u>No mistake</u>
   Ⓐ   Ⓑ   Ⓒ   Ⓓ

B. We have had a <u>successful</u> <u>business</u> for more than a <u>decade</u>. <u>No mistake</u>
              Ⓐ   Ⓑ   Ⓒ   Ⓓ

> **Tips and Reminders**
> - Eliminate any answer choices that you know are spelled correctly.
> - Apply the spelling rules that you know.
> - Check the spelling of any homophones (words that are pronounced the same but are spelled differently, such as *grown* and *groan*).
> - If you are not sure which word is misspelled, look for an answer choice that looks wrong or that you have never seen before.

PRACTICE

1. That <u>private</u> school is <u>amoung</u> the best in the <u>region</u>. <u>No mistake</u>
      Ⓐ   Ⓑ   Ⓒ   Ⓓ

2. <u>Although</u> there is an <u>abundance</u> of food, don't <u>waist</u> any. <u>No mistake</u>
   Ⓐ   Ⓑ   Ⓒ   Ⓓ

3. Our <u>foundasion</u> pays <u>scientists</u> who work in the <u>laboratory</u>. <u>No mistake</u>
      Ⓐ   Ⓑ   Ⓒ   Ⓓ

Go On ➡

4. What was the <u>approximate</u> time of your <u>nephew's</u> <u>arrival</u>? <u>No mistake</u>
         Ⓐ   Ⓑ   Ⓒ   Ⓓ

5. The <u>conductor</u> bowed when the <u>orchester</u> finished the <u>performance</u>. <u>No mistake</u>
    Ⓐ   Ⓑ   Ⓒ   Ⓓ

6. We knew <u>imeddiately</u> that the <u>journey</u> would be <u>dangerous</u>. <u>No mistake</u>
          Ⓐ   Ⓑ   Ⓒ   Ⓓ

7. The <u>museum</u> had several <u>pieces</u> of <u>jewlery</u> on display. <u>No mistake</u>
    Ⓐ   Ⓑ   Ⓒ   Ⓓ

8. <u>Patience</u> will get you <u>through</u> many <u>advenchures</u>. <u>No mistake</u>
   Ⓐ   Ⓑ   Ⓒ   Ⓓ

9. Charles <u>road</u> a <u>horse</u> in the <u>parade</u>. <u>No mistake</u>
        Ⓐ Ⓑ   Ⓒ   Ⓓ

10. This <u>foreign</u> word is <u>dificult</u> to <u>pronounce</u>. <u>No mistake</u>
     Ⓐ   Ⓑ   Ⓒ   Ⓓ

11. Jerry <u>couldn't</u> <u>appraoch</u> the <u>goal.</u> <u>No mistake</u>
     Ⓐ   Ⓑ   Ⓒ   Ⓓ

12. My dog looks <u>guilty</u> when he does <u>annything</u> <u>wrong</u>. <u>No mistake</u>
           Ⓐ   Ⓑ   Ⓒ   Ⓓ

13. The <u>victom</u> has been <u>unconscious</u> <u>since</u> Tuesday. <u>No mistake</u>
     Ⓐ   Ⓑ   Ⓒ   Ⓓ

14. The <u>jury</u> <u>decided</u> that the woman was <u>innocent</u>. <u>No mistake</u>
     Ⓐ Ⓑ   Ⓒ   Ⓓ

15. Meg <u>soaked</u> the floor when she <u>rung</u> out the <u>washcloth</u>. <u>No mistake</u>
    Ⓐ   Ⓑ   Ⓒ   Ⓓ

Stop

Mathematics

PRACTICE 18 • Computation

Directions: Find the answer to each problem. If the correct answer is not given, fill in the bubble for N, "Not Given."

SAMPLES

A. $342 \times 7 =$

    Ⓐ 2194
    Ⓑ 2384
    Ⓒ 2394
    Ⓓ N

C. $525 \div 25 =$

    Ⓐ 20
    Ⓑ 22
    Ⓒ 25
    Ⓓ N

B. $\begin{array}{r} \$8.30 \\ -\ 6.39 \\ \hline \end{array}$

    Ⓐ $1.91
    Ⓑ $2.01
    Ⓒ $2.91
    Ⓓ N

D. $\frac{1}{8} + \frac{3}{8} =$

    Ⓐ 4
    Ⓑ $\frac{1}{2}$
    Ⓒ $\frac{4}{16}$
    Ⓓ N

Tips and Reminders

- Look at the sign to see if you need to add (+), subtract (−), multiply (×), or divide (÷ or ⌐), and check your answer.

- When you work with fractions, be sure to simplify your answer.

- When using decimal numbers, check your answer carefully to make sure the decimal point is in the right place.

PRACTICE

1. $\begin{array}{r} 23 \\ 16 \\ 38 \\ +\ 54 \\ \hline \end{array}$

    Ⓐ 121
    Ⓑ 131
    Ⓒ 231
    Ⓓ N

2. $\begin{array}{r} \frac{3}{4} \\ -\ \frac{1}{4} \\ \hline \end{array}$

    Ⓐ $\frac{3}{4}$
    Ⓑ $\frac{1}{4}$
    Ⓒ $\frac{2}{8}$
    Ⓓ N

Go On →

3. 530
  $\times\,60$

Ⓐ 1800
Ⓑ 3180
Ⓒ 31,800
Ⓓ N

10. 6 + 245 + 39 =

Ⓐ 270
Ⓑ 290
Ⓒ 544
Ⓓ N

4. 211 ÷ 13 =

Ⓐ 15 R6
Ⓑ 16
Ⓒ 16 R3
Ⓓ N

11. 6.2 − 4.1 =

Ⓐ 21
Ⓑ 2.3
Ⓒ 2.1
Ⓓ N

5. 941
  − 728

Ⓐ 213
Ⓑ 223
Ⓒ 123
Ⓓ N

12. 1.34 × 2 =

Ⓐ 26.8
Ⓑ 2.68
Ⓒ 0.268
Ⓓ N

6. $\frac{3}{12} + \frac{5}{12} =$

Ⓐ $\frac{2}{3}$
Ⓑ $\frac{8}{24}$
Ⓒ $\frac{5}{12}$
Ⓓ N

13. $0.5\overline{)25}$

Ⓐ 5
Ⓑ 50
Ⓒ 500
Ⓓ N

14. $\frac{3}{9} + \frac{2}{9} =$

Ⓐ $\frac{5}{9}$
Ⓑ $\frac{5}{18}$
Ⓒ $\frac{5}{81}$
Ⓓ N

7. 300 × 10 =

Ⓐ 300
Ⓑ 3000
Ⓒ 30,000
Ⓓ N

8. $6\overline{)234}$

Ⓐ 39 R2
Ⓑ 38
Ⓒ 38 R5
Ⓓ N

15. 0.9 − 0.6 =

Ⓐ 0.003
Ⓑ 0.03
Ⓒ 3
Ⓓ N

9. $159.60
  − 82.95

Ⓐ $242.55
Ⓑ $77.65
Ⓒ $76.55
Ⓓ N

16. 47
  $\times\,22$

Ⓐ 188
Ⓑ 934
Ⓒ 1034
Ⓓ N

Go On

17. $0.6 \times 0.3 =$

(A) 0.18
(B) 1.8
(C) 18.0
(D) N

18. $\begin{array}{r} \$762.50 \\ + 48.20 \end{array}$

(A) $710.70
(B) $714.30
(C) $810.70
(D) N

19. $\begin{array}{r} 0.34 \\ 0.23 \\ + 0.46 \end{array}$

(A) 0.103
(B) 0.93
(C) 1.03
(D) N

20. $\frac{7}{8} - \frac{1}{4} =$

(A) $\frac{6}{8}$
(B) $\frac{5}{8}$
(C) 1
(D) N

21. $15\overline{)965}$

(A) 64
(B) 64 R10
(C) 65
(D) N

22. $0.354 + 2.3 =$

(A) 2.654
(B) 0.6194
(C) 0.377
(D) N

23. $\frac{1}{2} \times \frac{2}{3} =$

(A) $\frac{1}{3}$
(B) $\frac{7}{6}$
(C) $\frac{3}{6}$
(D) N

24. $38 \times 500 =$

(A) 1900
(B) 19,000
(C) 19,500
(D) N

25. $\$9.37 - \$0.62 =$

(A) $8.65
(B) $8.85
(C) $9.65
(D) N

26. $4 \div \frac{1}{5} =$

(A) $\frac{4}{5}$
(B) 20
(C) $\frac{20}{5}$
(D) N

27. $\frac{5}{8} + \frac{5}{8} =$

(A) $\frac{8}{10}$
(B) $\frac{25}{64}$
(C) $1\frac{1}{4}$
(D) N

28. $\begin{array}{r} 2374 \\ - 1506 \end{array}$

(A) 866
(B) 878
(C) 1868
(D) N

29. $0.3 \times 0.7 =$

(A) 0.21
(B) 2.1
(C) 21.0
(D) N

30. $4.5 \div 3 =$

(A) 15
(B) 1.5
(C) 1.05
(D) N

Stop

Reading

PRACTICE 19 • Inferences

SAMPLE

Directions: Read this passage about a girl named Sandra. Then answer the questions below.

As she sat before the huge oak desk, Sandra could hear water dripping from the roof outside. She would not be playing soccer today. With a long, drawn-out sigh, Sandra stared at the globe on the desk and noticed a single island in the Pacific Ocean. "It would be fun to go there," she thought.

Suddenly, Sandra could feel the sand between her toes and hear the crash of the waves. Three dolphins leaped out of the greenish blue water as they made their way into the lagoon. Sandra turned to her best friend, Laura. She was about to speak when she caught the scent of homemade soup.

"Sandra, the soup is ready," her father called from the kitchen.

"Okay, I'll be right there." Sandra looked once again at the tiny island on the globe. Then she turned and left the room.

A. Where is Sandra?

  Ⓐ on an island

  Ⓑ at school

  Ⓒ in her father's study

  Ⓓ on a ship

B. Why wasn't Sandra going to play soccer?

  Ⓐ She did not feel well.

  Ⓑ Her father would not let her.

  Ⓒ She had to do her homework.

  Ⓓ It was raining.

C. What will Sandra probably do next?

  Ⓐ eat lunch

  Ⓑ go outside

  Ⓒ walk along the beach

  Ⓓ study the globe

Tips and Reminders

- To make inferences or predictions, look for clues in the passage.
- Check each answer choice to decide which is most likely.
- When you draw a conclusion or make a generalization, make sure that the information in the passage supports it.

Go On →

PRACTICE

Directions: Read this passage about Paul's experiences at the mall. Then answer questions 1–4.

Paul's mother was getting her hair done in the salon at the mall. "Meet me here at exactly 4:30," she said. "And no leaving the mall!" she added, as if he was still five years old. The hairdresser smiled.

In a store called Little Russia, Paul picked up a tiny box with a princess painted on the lid. The price was $135.00. Paul replaced the box and fled, relieved that the girl behind the counter was ignoring him.

Next door was the Bath Shop. Paul forced himself to go in. Nervously, he picked up a sample jar of pale greenish goo and dabbed some on his hand. It smelled disgusting! He escaped just as a saleswoman approached him.

In Babbington Tools, Paul searched for a nice, inexpensive kitchen utensil. But as he fumbled through the hundreds of objects on display, he realized that he didn't recognize one of them. Paul sweated, afraid that some salesperson would ask him what he wanted. He left empty-handed.

His watch said 4:25. If he didn't get back in time, his mother would be sure he'd been kidnapped. But her birthday was tomorrow! Paul hurried past the hair salon and ducked into Clea's Cute Cards.

1. What is Paul looking for at the mall?

   Ⓐ a gift for his mother

   Ⓑ a treat for himself

   Ⓒ a present for the hairdresser

   Ⓓ a gift for a friend

2. What happens to Paul in each store that he visits?

   Ⓐ He finds objects that are too expensive.

   Ⓑ The salesperson ignores him.

   Ⓒ He feels embarrassed.

   Ⓓ He buys something.

3. Which word best describes how Paul's mother feels toward him?

   Ⓐ selfish

   Ⓑ protective

   Ⓒ jealous

   Ⓓ ashamed

4. What will Paul most likely do next?

   Ⓐ go back to the Bath Shop

   Ⓑ hide from his mother

   Ⓒ buy a birthday card

   Ⓓ ask his mother for advice

Go On

Directions: Read this passage about our national forests. Then answer questions 5–8.

Our national forests were established in 1897. The U.S. government set them aside to protect the forests and to provide a supply of timber for the nation. One hundred years later, many Americans still see the national forests as a rich source of lumber. Others believe that all our national forests should be left untouched. Today, the United States National Forest System consists of 191 million acres. Timber harvesting is permitted on only 49 million of those acres.

Some Americans believe that the forests should be used primarily for the enjoyment of recreational visitors. On weekends, for example, city-dwellers pour into the forests outside Atlanta and Seattle, where they fill the air with music and smoke from campfires. The San Bernardino Forest outside Los Angeles is littered with trash left there by visitors. In Oregon, sightseers roar along the remote Rogue River in motorboats. Some environmentalists think that limits should be placed on how many visitors can visit a national forest at one time.

Attitudes have changed over the past 100 years. Americans who once thought that the forests were vast and unchanging now think they are shrinking.

5. What conclusions about our national forests can be drawn from this passage?

Ⓐ Timber harvesting occurs on a small portion of forest lands.

Ⓑ Every city has a national forest.

Ⓒ National forests are only for recreation.

Ⓓ The forests are in better shape now than when they were created.

6. What do all the recreational visitors described here have in common?

Ⓐ They disturb the peace and beauty of the forests.

Ⓑ They leave trash behind.

Ⓒ They make a lot of noise.

Ⓓ They think the forests should be harvested for timber.

7. From this passage, you can conclude that –

Ⓐ few Americans value our forests

Ⓑ Americans cannot agree on how best to manage the forests

Ⓒ most Americans don't even know about our national forests

Ⓓ most Americans think the forests should be left alone

8. In the future, Americans most likely will –

Ⓐ destroy all the forests

Ⓑ stop visiting forests

Ⓒ be more careful with our forests

Ⓓ stop using timber

Go On

Directions: Read this passage about a sixth-grade class. Then answer questions 9–14 on the next page.

Mr. Chiu brought to class a statistic stating that American kids aged 6–11 watch over nineteen hours of television per week.

"This is terrible!" he exclaimed. "Why are you kids filling your heads with this junk instead of doing something useful?"

"We aren't just watching junk," protested Sam. "A lot of the stuff we watch is on educational channels. Besides, I know my friends and I do a lot of other things besides watching TV. I don't think I watch over 19 hours a week."

"Neither do I!" said Jessica. Everybody else chimed in.

"Okay," said Mr. Chiu, "I challenge all of you in class to monitor your TV viewing habits for a month. You'll have to record how much you watch, what you watch, and what other activities you get involved in during your leisure time. This could be interesting."

The class accepted the challenge. Using the class computer, they created weekly viewing logs for each student to take home. They divided themselves into four groups. Each group was responsible for making sure that its members filled in their viewing log each day. Students also received journals in which to jot down other activities, such as sports, crafts, computer games, playing with pets, and so on.

At the end of the month, each group presented its results. One person in each group presented a report, and each group summarized its results in bar graphs.

Based on the results for the whole class, the students discovered that every student watched an average of 22 hours of TV per week. For about one-quarter of the time they spent watching TV, the students watched nature programs, foreign-language instruction programs, and other educational shows. The rest of the time was spent watching shows that were pure entertainment.

The students also determined how much time they spent on other activities. Across the entire class, students averaged 6 hours a week playing sports or getting other forms of exercise, 2 hours a week reading, 8 hours a week playing with friends, and 12 hours a week on the computer, playing games or on the Internet.

After the students presented their findings, Mr. Chiu looked thoughtful.

"Well," he said, "it's time to look more carefully at these numbers. What do they tell you?"

Go On →

9. From this passage, you can infer that Mr. Chiu thinks –

   Ⓐ sports are less valuable than reading

   Ⓑ watching TV has little or no value

   Ⓒ his students will not tell the truth about their viewing habits

   Ⓓ educational TV is a great learning tool

10. At the beginning of this story, Sam thinks that –

   Ⓐ he and his friends are being unfairly accused by their teacher

   Ⓑ he watches less TV than his classmates

   Ⓒ educational TV is junk

   Ⓓ watching a lot of TV is something to be proud of

11. Which statement about Mr. Chiu's students is most likely true?

   Ⓐ They do not like to read.

   Ⓑ They watch more educational TV than entertainment TV.

   Ⓒ They spend more hours playing on the computer than doing anything else.

   Ⓓ They spend more time watching TV than exercising.

12. What inference can you make about Mr. Chiu's teaching style?

   Ⓐ He carefully plans all of his lessons months ahead of time.

   Ⓑ He runs the classroom without student input.

   Ⓒ He encourages students to think for themselves.

   Ⓓ He is not very interested in his students' thoughts and lives.

13. What conclusion can be drawn about the statistic that Mr. Chiu brings to class?

   Ⓐ It is absolutely correct.

   Ⓑ It is definitely incorrect.

   Ⓒ It is supported by the data from Mr. Chiu's class.

   Ⓓ It is not supported by the data from Mr. Chiu's class.

14. What will most likely happen next?

   Ⓐ Mr. Chiu will show that the students' data is incorrect.

   Ⓑ Mr. Chiu will have the students study other statistics about American youth.

   Ⓒ Mr. Chiu will ask students to repeat the numbers to him.

   Ⓓ Mr. Chiu and the students will try to draw conclusions from the data.

Stop

Language Arts

PRACTICE 20 • Combining Sentences

SAMPLES

Directions: Read the two sentences in the box. Choose the best way to combine them to form one sentence.

A.
> The balloon was scarlet and black.
> It rose into the air.

  Ⓐ The balloon, it was scarlet and black, rose into the air.

  Ⓑ The balloon rose like scarlet and black into the air.

  Ⓒ The balloon rose into the air, although it was scarlet and black.

  Ⓓ The scarlet and black balloon rose into the air.

Directions: Read the paragraph and answer the question that follows.

> Every Wednesday, Isaac and Josiah walk to the public library where they do their homework. At 5:15, their dad picks them up and takes them out to a restaurant. During dinner they play 20 Questions. This is a guessing game.

B. Which is the best way to combine the last two sentences?

  Ⓐ During dinner this is what they play, the 20 Questions guessing game.

  Ⓑ During dinner they play a guessing game 20 Questions.

  Ⓒ During dinner they play 20 Questions, a guessing game.

  Ⓓ During dinner 20 Questions they play, a guessing game.

Tips and Reminders

- Check the order of words in the combined sentence to make sure it is correct.

- Make sure the combined sentence has the same meaning as the two original sentences.

- Be careful in using conjunctions and connecting words, such as *but, so,* and *although.* Using an incorrect conjunction can change the meaning of the sentence.

Go On →

PRACTICE

Directions: Read the two sentences in the box. Choose the best way to combine them to form one sentence.

1. The fans were excited.
   The fans cheered for the home team.

   (A) The fans were excited, but they cheered for the home team.
   (B) The excited fans cheered for the home team.
   (C) The fans cheered for the excited home team.
   (D) The fans, who were excited, they cheered for the home team.

2. Skateboards are on sale at GoSports.
   Inline skates are on sale there, too.

   (A) Skateboards and inline skates are on sale at GoSports.
   (B) Skateboards are on sale at GoSports, but inline skates are, too.
   (C) GoSports sells both skateboards and inline skates on sale.
   (D) Skateboards are on sale, too.

3. The train has a whistle.
   The whistle blows at each station.

   (A) The train has a whistle for each station.
   (B) The train has a whistle that blows.
   (C) The whistle blows at each station.
   (D) The train's whistle blows at each station.

4. Uncle Jerry is my mother's brother.
   Uncle Jerry is a teacher.

   (A) Uncle Jerry is a teacher.
   (B) Uncle Jerry is my mother's brother, and he is a teacher.
   (C) Uncle Jerry, my mother's brother, is a teacher.
   (D) Uncle Jerry is my mother's teacher.

5. Jenny leaped into the air.
   Jenny headed the ball into the net.

   (A) Jenny leaped into the air and headed the ball into the net.
   (B) Jenny leaped and headed the ball.
   (C) Jenny, who leaped, headed the ball.
   (D) Jenny leaped and headed the ball into the air.

6. The loons paddled across the water.
   The loons made a mournful cry.

   (A) The loons, while they paddled across the water, they made a mournful cry.
   (B) The loons paddled across the water, and the loons made a mournful cry.
   (C) As the loons paddled across the water, they made a mournful cry.
   (D) Although the loons paddled across the water, they made a mournful cry.

Go On

Directions: Read each paragraph. Then answer the questions that follow.

Paragraph 1

Thank you so much for inviting me! Thank you for inviting me to stay for ten whole days! I loved the trips to Roger Williams Zoo and the Mystic Aquarium. I didn't mind your new puppy. I didn't mind that it ate my old shoes!

---

7. Which is the best way to combine the first two sentences?

Ⓐ Thank you so much for inviting me I stayed for ten whole days!

Ⓑ Thank you so much for ten whole days for inviting me.

Ⓒ Thank you so much for inviting me to stay for ten whole days!

Ⓓ Thank you so much because you invited me and I stayed for ten days!

8. Which is the best way to combine the last two sentences?

Ⓐ I didn't mind that your new puppy ate my old shoes!

Ⓑ I didn't mind your new puppy it ate my old shoes!

Ⓒ Your new puppy ate my old shoes, and I didn't mind that it ate them!

Ⓓ Your new puppy eating my old shoes and me not minding.

Paragraph 2

Long ago, people lived in that lighthouse. It is near Carmel. The lighthouse keeper and his family stayed there year round. Several children were born there. Carolina LeMott was born in the lighthouse.

---

9. Which is the best way to combine the first two sentences?

Ⓐ Long ago, people who lived in that lighthouse lived near Carmel.

Ⓑ Long ago, people lived in that lighthouse near Carmel.

Ⓒ Long ago, there lived in that lighthouse some people near Carmel.

Ⓓ The long-ago people who lived in that lighthouse were near Carmel.

10. Which is the best way to combine the last two sentences?

Ⓐ Several children were born there, and Carolina LeMott was born there.

Ⓑ Several children, one of them was Carolina LeMott, were born there.

Ⓒ Carolina LeMott was born there and several children also.

Ⓓ Several children, including Carolina LeMott, were born in the lighthouse.

Stop

Mathematics

PRACTICE 21 • Estimation

Directions: Choose the best answer to each question.

SAMPLES

A. Which is the closest estimate of 219×95?

- Ⓐ 300×100
- Ⓑ 200×150
- Ⓒ 200×100
- Ⓓ 200×50

B. The closest estimate of $3248 - 1602$ is –

- Ⓐ 1800
- Ⓑ 1600
- Ⓒ 1400
- Ⓓ 1200

> **Tips and Reminders**
> - To estimate, use rounding or estimating with compatible numbers.
> - Use number sense to check your answer.

PRACTICE

1.

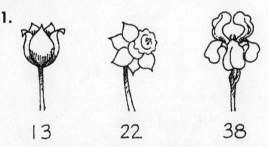

13   22   38

Which numbers give the best estimate of the total number of flowers?

- Ⓐ $20 + 20 + 30$
- Ⓑ $10 + 20 + 30$
- Ⓒ $10 + 30 + 40$
- Ⓓ $10 + 20 + 40$

2. The closest estimate of $29{,}093 + 68{,}745$ is –

- Ⓐ 1,000,000
- Ⓑ 100,000
- Ⓒ 10,000
- Ⓓ 1000

3. If one pair of socks costs $1.85, what is the closest estimate of the cost for 5 pairs of socks?

- Ⓐ $5.00
- Ⓑ $7.50
- Ⓒ $10.00
- Ⓓ $12.00

Go On

PRACTICE 21 • Estimation (continued)

4. The closest estimate of $31.98 × 8 is –

Ⓐ $240.00

Ⓑ $320.00

Ⓒ $480.00

Ⓓ $560.00

5. Which is the closest estimate of 3211 – 2689?

Ⓐ 400

Ⓑ 500

Ⓒ 600

Ⓓ 700

6. The closest estimate of 4230 ÷ 71 is between –

Ⓐ 50 and 60

Ⓑ 60 and 70

Ⓒ 70 and 80

Ⓓ 80 and 90

7. Which is the closest estimate of $0.13 × 60?

Ⓐ $7.00

Ⓑ $8.00

Ⓒ $70.00

Ⓓ $80.00

8. Which is the closest estimate of 67,214 + 10,895?

Ⓐ 70,000

Ⓑ 75,000

Ⓒ 80,000

Ⓓ 85,000

9.

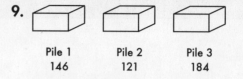

| Pile 1 | Pile 2 | Pile 3 |
| 146 | 121 | 184 |

Which numbers would give the closest estimate of the total number of bricks?

Ⓐ 150 + 120 + 180

Ⓑ 140 + 120 + 180

Ⓒ 150 + 130 + 190

Ⓓ 140 + 130 + 190

10. Which is the closest estimate of 103,443 – 9765?

Ⓐ 90,000

Ⓑ 80,000

Ⓒ 9000

Ⓓ 8000

11. 6380 ÷ 8 is between –

Ⓐ 60 and 70

Ⓑ 70 and 80

Ⓒ 600 and 700

Ⓓ 700 and 800

12. Which numbers would give the best estimate of $8\frac{1}{6} + 7\frac{5}{8} + 3\frac{1}{8}$?

Ⓐ 8 + 8 + 4

Ⓑ 8 + 8 + 3

Ⓒ 7 + 7 + 4

Ⓓ 7 + 7 + 3

Stop

Reading

PRACTICE 22 • Literary Elements

SAMPLES

Directions: Read this story about what happened to the animals. Then answer questions A and B.

Long ago, all the creatures of the world got together and decided that the sun should shine all the time. Only one creature, the owl, disagreed. "Darkness is good," declared the owl. "It is the necessary opposite of light. Besides, I hunt best in the dark." But everyone ignored Owl, and the world became a place of perpetual sunlight.

At first the creatures were immensely pleased. However, after a while, they began to grow irritable, dull, and unhappy. "What is wrong with us?" they moaned. "We hate this life."

"You're tired," pronounced the owl. "You need some sleep, foolish creatures, and for that you need darkness. I'll see if I can get things changed."

Owl did get things changed, and the days were divided into half light and half dark. All the creatures, except one, slept at night, woke refreshed, and enjoyed life again. And the wise owl hunted undisturbed while they slept.

A. This story would most likely be found in a collection of

- Ⓐ fairy tales
- Ⓑ stories about life in the past
- Ⓒ folk tales
- Ⓓ science fiction stories

B. The theme of this story suggests that

- Ⓐ most animals are lazy
- Ⓑ individuals often don't know what is best for them
- Ⓒ the world is a cruel place
- Ⓓ what is good for one creature is good for all

Tips and Reminders
- Look back at the passage to answer questions about details.
- For other questions, you may need to "read between the lines." Think about the story and what you already know to answer these questions.

Go On

PRACTICE

Directions: Read this story about a sixth-grade field trip. Then answer questions 1–7 on the next page.

On the day of the field trip to Old Burbridge Village, three enormous buses were lined up at the curb at 7:15. As car after car pulled into the parking lot, kids waved good-bye to their parents and munched on half-finished breakfast foods.

Mary Lecjiewski was assigned to Bus 1. She had arrived before anyone else, carrying her portable CD player, the inhaler for her asthma, her sunscreen, a lunchbox full of treats, her sun hat, some board games with magnetic pieces, a camera, and her diary. She saved a seat for her best friend, Shavawn Greene.

At 7:25, Ms. Kotrubash, the parent volunteer for Bus 1, was pacing the aisle holding a clipboard and checking names on a piece of paper. She looked at her watch and then, with a frantic expression, began to recheck the names.

"If you're looking for Shavawn Greene," said Mary as she neatly placed her jacket in the luggage rack, "she'll be here in five and a half minutes."

"How do you know?" asked Ms. Kotrubash.

"Because," said Mary, "Shavawn has been in my class since kindergarten. For the first-grade field trip, she arrived five minutes before the bus left. In second grade, she arrived four minutes before the scheduled departure. In third grade she had three minutes to spare, in fourth grade two minutes, and in fifth grade one minute. This year–"

"Well, we can't wait even one minute this year," said Ms. Kotrubash, looking very unhappy. "The principal said so."

By 7:29, everyone on the bus was eagerly looking out the window. As the seconds swept toward 7:30, a small brown station wagon pulled into the parking lot. Shavawn got out, looking totally relaxed, and climbed onto the bus, smiling and waving like royalty as her classmates cheered.

"Next time try to arrive a little earlier, Shavawn," sputtered Ms. Kotrubash.

"What do you have for lunch?" asked Shavawn as she squeezed in next to Mary. "I bet it will be yummy! We left in kind of a hurry this morning."

"I figured that," nodded Mary. "So I packed two lunches plus a breakfast bar for you. How about a game of chess when you finish eating?"

Go On

1. Where does this story take place?

   Ⓐ at Old Burbridge Village

   Ⓑ outside Shavawn's house

   Ⓒ outside Mary's house

   Ⓓ in a school parking lot

2. What is the main conflict in the first part of the story?

   Ⓐ Shavawn has not appeared, but the bus must leave at 7:30.

   Ⓑ Mary is angry, but Shavawn still wants to be her friend.

   Ⓒ Mary wants to go on the trip but also wants to stay with Shavawn.

   Ⓓ Mary feels loyal to Shavawn, but the other students dislike Shavawn.

3. The climax of the story occurs when

   Ⓐ Mary gets on the bus

   Ⓑ Ms. Kotrubash realizes that someone is missing

   Ⓒ Shavawn arrives

   Ⓓ Ms. Kotrubash scolds Shavawn

4. Which words best describe Mary?

   Ⓐ stiff and unfriendly

   Ⓑ organized but relaxed

   Ⓒ tense and worried

   Ⓓ messy but confident

5. How did Shavawn feel at the end of the story?

   Ⓐ ashamed for arriving late

   Ⓑ unaware that she had arrived last

   Ⓒ pleased with the way things had worked out

   Ⓓ fearful that Mary was upset with her

6. This story is an example of what kind of literature?

   Ⓐ realistic fiction

   Ⓑ historical fiction

   Ⓒ science fiction

   Ⓓ mystery story

7. The tone of this story is best described as

   Ⓐ sad and moody

   Ⓑ light and relaxed

   Ⓒ bitter and angry

   Ⓓ wild and silly

Go On

Directions: Read this story about the man in Apartment 2B. Then answer questions 8–11.

A storm lashed the windows of the apartment building. Inside Apartment 2B, a man sat huddled in an armchair, still dressed in a coat and hat. Raindrops dripped slowly off the brim of his hat and splashed onto the chair, briefly turning the faded reds and yellows of the fabric bright again. The man did not move.

He hunched forward, staring at the dusty gray carpet. His whole body looked tired and defeated, except for his bony hands, which clutched a small paper bag tightly as if it were the most valuable thing on Earth.

A clock ticked loudly. The man ignored it.

The afternoon wore on, and the room grew darker, but the man did not get up to switch on a light. At 4:32, the phone rang, shattering the stillness. The man twitched, an expression of fear on his face, but he did not get up.

Twenty rings, thirty . . . finally the ringing stopped, and the man's face relaxed slightly. But a minute later, something else rang.

"The doorbell!" cried the man out loud. Frantically, he stumbled about the room as if searching for something. Finally, he stuffed the bag under the chair cushion and went to answer the door.

8. Which sentence best summarizes the plot of this story?

   Ⓐ A storm rages outside an apartment building.

   Ⓑ Rain soaks the rug in a man's apartment.

   Ⓒ A man is waiting for something to happen.

   Ⓓ A man finds a bag and takes it home.

9. What is the mood of this story?

   Ⓐ tense

   Ⓑ lively

   Ⓒ tender

   Ⓓ calm

10. At the end of the story, the man's problem is how to

   Ⓐ get out of the apartment without being seen

   Ⓑ hide the bag from the person at the door

   Ⓒ find the object that is missing in his apartment

   Ⓓ answer the door and the telephone at the same time

11. The man in this story is best described as

   Ⓐ fearful

   Ⓑ cruel

   Ⓒ greedy

   Ⓓ clever

Stop

Language Arts

PRACTICE 23 • Composition

SAMPLE

Directions: Read this draft of a report. Then answer questions A and B.

They have burglar alarms, CD players, and coffee machines set to go off
(1)
or on at certain times of day. Many people have timers on the lights in
(2)
their houses. When they are away, lamps automatically switch on and off at
(3)
night to scare off intruders. My little sister likes to turn lights off and on, too.
(4)

A. Which topic sentence would best begin this paragraph?

Ⓐ Lights should be turned off and on often.

Ⓑ Is your house protected from burglars?

Ⓒ Some homeowners have complex home electronic systems.

Ⓓ Why not program your own home?

B. Which sentence does **not** belong in this report?

Ⓐ sentence 1

Ⓑ sentence 2

Ⓒ sentence 3

Ⓓ sentence 4

Tips and Reminders

• The topic sentence should tell what the whole paragraph is about. Every sentence in that paragraph should support the topic.

• To determine the writer's purpose or audience, think about what the writer is trying to say and to whom.

• When revising sentences, choose the answer that has the same meaning as the original sentence.

PRACTICE

Directions: Read this draft of a report on aviator Bessie Coleman. Then answer questions 1–6 on the next page.

First, she was a woman. Second, she was an African American. Her family
(1)   (2)   (3)
was poor. Yet Coleman stubbornly held on to her dream.
        (4)

   Born into a family of 13 children in 1893, Bessie Coleman picked cotton
        (5)
when she was growing up in Texas. Texas joined the Confederacy during the
                                                (6)
Civil War in the 1860s. Eventually she moved to Chicago, where she heard
                        (7)
about an African American named Eugene Jacques Bullard. Bullard had
                                                          (8)
traveled to France and flown for the French army during World War I.

   Coleman applied to aviation school in the United States but was denied
      (9)
admission because of her race. Frustrated, Coleman went to France herself.
                              (10)
   When Coleman returned to the United States, it was still the early days of
      (11)
aviation. The public, which was eager to watch flying exhibitions. Daredevil
          (12)   (13)
pilots such as Coleman crisscrossed the country performing stunts for thrilled

audiences. Sadly, Coleman's plane crashed during a show, so she never
              (14)
realized her other dream of founding a flight school for African Americans.

Go On

1. Which is the best topic sentence for the first paragraph of this report?

   (A) Bessie Coleman, an African American, grew up in Texas.

   (B) There were few female pilots in those days.

   (C) Bessie Coleman faced serious obstacles to becoming a pilot.

   (D) The first airplane was built in 1903.

2. Which is the best way to rewrite sentence 3 to fit better with the rest of the paragraph?

   (A) And also, there was poverty in her background.

   (B) Bessie Coleman was poor when she was growing up.

   (C) The third obstacle, poverty, was also in her way.

   (D) Third, she came from a poor family.

3. The writer's main purpose in this report is to –

   (A) persuade people to become aviators like Coleman

   (B) describe the achievements of Bessie Coleman

   (C) explain how airplanes work

   (D) compare Coleman with Bullard

4. Which sentence does **not** belong in the second paragraph?

   (A) sentence 5

   (B) sentence 6

   (C) sentence 7

   (D) sentence 8

5. Which sentence could best be added to the end of the third paragraph after sentence 10?

   (A) There she became a licensed pilot.

   (B) She did not speak French well.

   (C) World War I had already ended.

   (D) She arrived in Paris.

6. Which is the best way to revise sentence 12?

   (A) There was an eager public to watch flying exhibitions.

   (B) The public was eager to watch flying exhibitions.

   (C) The public, which was eager, wanted to watch flying exhibitions.

   (D) The public wanted to watch eager pilots in flying exhibitions.

Go On

Directions: Read this first draft of a report about earthquakes. Then answer questions 7–8.

They cause millions of dollars of damage to buildings, roads, bridges, and
(1)
other property. They also kill and injure thousands of people.
(2)
    Scientists study earthquakes in an attempt to predict where and when they
(3)
are likely to occur next. Scientists have identified the geographical locations
(4)
where earthquakes happen most frequently. These places all exist in places
(5)
where underlying sections of the earth's crust rub against each other.

    One way to predict earthquakes is to observe the behavior of animals.
(6)
Before an earthquake, animals will do strange things. Ducks will refuse to go
(7)   (8)
into water, and rats may suddenly start to swarm up telephone poles.

7. Which would be the best topic sentence to begin this report?

Ⓐ Buildings are now designed to withstand earthquakes.

Ⓑ In 1975, Chinese officials evacuated everybody from a town in Manchuria.

Ⓒ A huge earthquake struck San Francisco in 1906.

Ⓓ Earthquakes are sudden, powerful movements inside the earth.

8. Which sentence could best be added to the end of the second paragraph after sentence 5?

Ⓐ The pressure from the constant rubbing causes earthquakes.

Ⓑ Architects and engineers build structures that will not collapse.

Ⓒ A terrible earthquake occurred in China in 1556.

Ⓓ Scientists measure earthquakes using the Richter scale.

Go On

Directions: Read this paragraph from a report about snakes. Then answer questions 9–12.

> They lack fur, feathers, legs, and wings. They lack external ears, and most
> (1)   (2)
> snakes have poor vision. Yet snakes are very successful animals because they
>   (3)
> have a variety of survival strategies. One of the prettiest snakes is the coral
>   (4)
> snake. They move at speeds of up to 19 kilometers per hour. They use keen
>   (5)   (6)
> senses of smell, touch, and temperature to avoid enemies and catch their
>
> prey. A snake's tongue works like a nose, picking up smells and using them
>   (7)
> to figure out what other creatures are near it and exactly where they are
>
> located.

9. Which is the best topic sentence for this paragraph?

   (A) Most people do not like snakes.

   (B) Snakes lack many things that other creatures have.

   (C) Many snakes are poisonous.

   (D) People say that snake meat tastes like chicken.

10. Which sentence does **not** belong in this paragraph?

   (A) sentence 2

   (B) sentence 3

   (C) sentence 4

   (D) sentence 5

11. The author probably wrote this report for people who –

   (A) are interested in nature

   (B) are afraid of snakes

   (C) live in places where there are snakes

   (D) enjoy going to zoos

12. Which sentence could best be added to the end of this paragraph after sentence 7?

   (A) A snake's body is quite narrow.

   (B) Snakes do not like cold weather.

   (C) Rattlesnakes are fascinating.

   (D) Snakes are extraordinary in many ways.

Mathematics

PRACTICE 24 • Interpreting Data

SAMPLES

Directions: The Bartons kept a record of low and high temperatures of the water in their pool. Use the table of their results to answer questions A and B.

Daily Temperatures (°F)

Day	Low	High
Monday	72	74
Tuesday	72	77
Wednesday	74	78
Thursday	76	81
Friday	78	83

A. On which day was the water warmest?

  Ⓐ Tuesday   Ⓒ Thursday

  Ⓑ Wednesday   Ⓓ Friday

B. If the pattern on this table continues, what would be the most likely high temperature on Saturday?

  Ⓐ 80°F   Ⓒ 85°F

  Ⓑ 82°F   Ⓓ 90°F

Tips and Reminders

- Use the graph or chart to find the answer to each question.
- After choosing an answer, read the question again to make sure you have answered it correctly.

PRACTICE

Directions: Use the graph to answer 1–2.

Boats Used on Crystal Lake

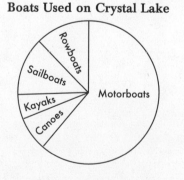

1. Which kind of boat is used least on Crystal Lake?

  Ⓐ rowboats   Ⓒ sailboats

  Ⓑ motorboats   Ⓓ kayaks

2. The majority of boats used on Crystal Lake are –

  Ⓐ canoes   Ⓒ sailboats

  Ⓑ motorboats   Ⓓ rowboats

Go On

PRACTICE 24 • Interpreting Data (continued)

Directions: This graph shows how many students have certain objects in their backpacks. Use the graph to answer 3–5.

Directions: This graph shows where students in grades 5 and 6 held their birthday parties last year. Use the graph to answer 6–7.

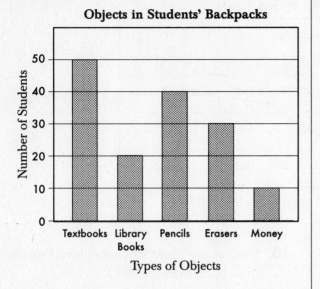

Objects in Students' Backpacks

Where Birthday Parties Were Held

3. How many students have erasers in their backpacks?

    Ⓐ 10   Ⓒ 25

    Ⓑ 20   Ⓓ 30

4. How many more students have pencils than library books?

    Ⓐ 5   Ⓒ 15

    Ⓑ 10   Ⓓ 20

5. Which of these was found in the least number of backpacks?

    Ⓐ money   Ⓒ pencils

    Ⓑ textbooks   Ⓓ erasers

6. How many students held their parties at a bowling alley?

    Ⓐ 10   Ⓒ 20

    Ⓑ 15   Ⓓ 25

7. The greatest number of parties were held at –

    Ⓐ students' homes

    Ⓑ movie theaters

    Ⓒ bowling alleys

    Ⓓ mini-golf centers

Go On

Directions: This graph shows how many sixth-grade students in Oak Brook participated in basketball and soccer in recent years. Use the graph to answer questions 8–11.

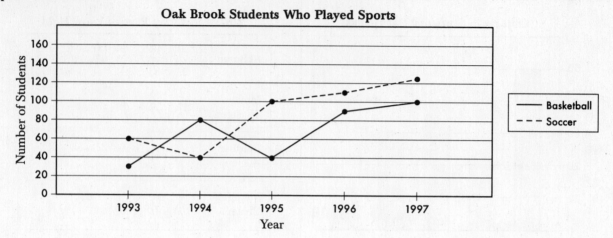

8. In what year did more students participate in basketball than in soccer?

   (A) 1993
   (B) 1994
   (C) 1995
   (D) 1996

9. How many students played soccer in 1997?

   (A) 100
   (B) 115
   (C) 120
   (D) 125

10. How many more students played soccer than basketball in 1997?

   (A) 115
   (B) 25
   (C) 15
   (D) 5

11. In which year did the fewest students play basketball?

   (A) 1993
   (B) 1994
   (C) 1995
   (D) 1996

PRACTICE 24 • Interpreting Data (continued)

Directions: This graph shows how many sixth-grade girls and boys passed the different parts of the Presidential Fitness Test. Use the graph to answer questions 12–13.

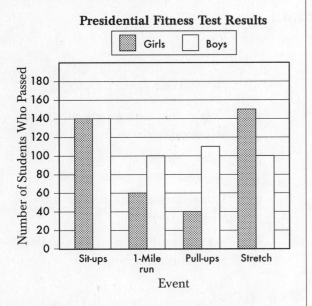

Presidential Fitness Test Results

Directions: This medical chart shows how Brendan's height compared with national averages over several years. Use the chart to answer questions 14–16.

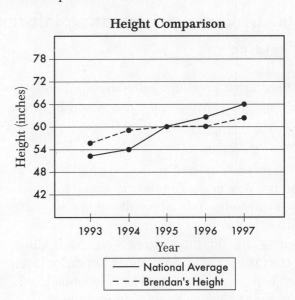

Height Comparison

12. Which part of the test did more girls pass than boys?

   Ⓐ Sit-ups   Ⓒ Pull-ups
   Ⓑ 1-Mile run   Ⓓ Stretch

13. How many more boys than girls passed the pull-ups test?

   Ⓐ 110   Ⓒ 60
   Ⓑ 70   Ⓓ 40

14. What was the average height for boys of Brendan's age in 1996?

   Ⓐ 54 in.   Ⓒ 60 in.
   Ⓑ 56 in.   Ⓓ 62 in.

15. How much taller than the national average was Brendan in 1993?

   Ⓐ 2 in.   Ⓒ 6 in.
   Ⓑ 4 in.   Ⓓ 8 in.

16. What can you conclude about Brendan's height in 1996–1997?

   Ⓐ He was taller than average.
   Ⓑ He grew rapidly.
   Ⓒ He was of average height.
   Ⓓ He was shorter than average.

Reading

PRACTICE 25 • Evaluating Information

SAMPLES

Directions: Read this letter about Valley Street. Then answer questions A and B.

To the Editor:

Every afternoon I walk along Valley Street on my way home from work. I used to look forward to this part of my day. After all, Valley Street has some of the prettiest views in the whole city. But these days a walk down Valley Street is terrifying. Sometimes I'm lucky just to get home in one piece. Why? Skateboarders have made Valley Street a danger zone.

I really don't want to spoil young skateboarders' fun, but a sidewalk is not the place for zipping around on a speedy skateboard. Older people like me have trouble getting out of the way. I've already seen a dozen close calls. Luckily, no one has been badly hurt—yet! Before a serious accident does happen, let's get skateboards off our sidewalks!

Mary Lou Inness

A. Which sentence states a fact?

(A) Every afternoon I walk along Valley Street on my way home from work.

(B) Valley Street has some of the prettiest views in the whole city.

(C) These days a walk down Valley Street is terrifying.

(D) Skateboarders have made Valley Street a danger zone.

B. Which sentence is intended to persuade readers that the Valley Street skateboarders are dangerous?

(A) I don't want to spoil young skateboarders' fun.

(B) Valley Street has some of the prettiest views in the city.

(C) Older people like me have trouble getting out of the way.

(D) Luckily, no one has been badly hurt—yet!

Tips and Reminders

• A fact is a statement that can be proven true. An opinion is a statement, belief, or feeling that cannot be proven true.

• For questions about techniques of persuasion, think carefully about what the author is trying to say. Look for statements or claims made without any supporting evidence.

Go On

PRACTICE

Directions: Choose the best answer to each question.

1. Which statement about computers is an opinion?

   Ⓐ In recent years, computers have improved our lives.

   Ⓑ A computer is a machine that stores information the user puts into it.

   Ⓒ The first computers were larger but less powerful than today's.

   Ⓓ A "bug" is a problem that can keep a computer from working.

2. Which statement about a candidate for mayor of Mapleton is most persuasive?

   Ⓐ Elena Ferrante has new ideas for Mapleton.

   Ⓑ Elena Ferrante was born and raised in Mapleton.

   Ⓒ Elena Ferrante has served on the Mapleton city council for six years.

   Ⓓ Elena Ferrante has always wanted to be mayor of Mapleton.

3. Which statement about sports is an opinion?

   Ⓐ Soccer and football are team sports.

   Ⓑ Running and bicycling require strong leg muscles.

   Ⓒ Hockey is the most difficult sport.

   Ⓓ Tennis and volleyball are played with a net.

4. Which statement about gardening is a fact?

   Ⓐ Buy gardening tools that have handles made of wood, not plastic.

   Ⓑ A border of flowers adds charm to a vegetable garden.

   Ⓒ Planting seeds too close together is the worst mistake you can make.

   Ⓓ Some plants grow well in shade, while others need direct sunlight.

5. Which statement tries to convince you to buy a toothpaste because it is better than other brands?

   Ⓐ Actress Tia Sherman says, "Dentaguard Toothpaste keeps my teeth white."

   Ⓑ Four out of five dentists recommend Dentaguard for their patients.

   Ⓒ Clean your teeth and save money with Dentaguard.

   Ⓓ Dentaguard's great flavor makes brushing a pleasure.

6. Which statement about eating is an opinion?

   Ⓐ Food that is good for you usually does not taste as good as junk food.

   Ⓑ If you eat more food than your body uses, you will gain weight.

   Ⓒ To stay healthy, it is important to eat a well-balanced diet.

   Ⓓ Cheese, meat, fish, and eggs contain protein that your body needs.

Go On

Directions: Read the newspaper article about a clean-up campaign. Then answer questions 7–9.

Volunteers Needed for Clean-up

Volunteers are needed for Lake County's Fifth Annual Spring Clean-up. The Clean-up is scheduled for this Saturday. Director Lee Farnsworth estimates that 200 volunteers will be needed. They will be assigned to teams and work in four-hour shifts. Clean-up jobs will include picking up road trash, raking leaves, and painting park benches.

In the last four years, volunteers have made the Spring Clean-up a great success. As Director Farnsworth says, "If you love Lake County, volunteering is the best way to show it. And when our streets and parks look good, we all feel better." In case of heavy rain, the Clean-up will be postponed. But Director Farnsworth hopes a few sprinkles won't discourage anyone. "When you're working for a good cause, a little water shouldn't bother you," he laughs.

7. This newspaper article tries to interest people in volunteering by suggesting that the work is –

   (A) fun and exciting

   (B) important and rewarding

   (C) glamorous and interesting

   (D) easy and relaxing

8. Which sentence from this article states an opinion?

   (A) Volunteers are needed for Lake County's Fifth Annual Spring Clean-up.

   (B) The Clean-up is scheduled for this Saturday.

   (C) If you love Lake County, volunteering is the best way to show it.

   (D) In case of heavy rain, the Clean-up will be postponed.

9. Which sentence states a fact?

   (A) Clean-up jobs will include picking up trash and raking leaves.

   (B) Volunteers have made the Spring Clean-up a great success.

   (C) And when our streets and parks look good, we all feel better.

   (D) When you're working for a good cause, a little water shouldn't bother you.

Go On

Directions: Read the advertisement for jeans. Then answer questions 10–12.

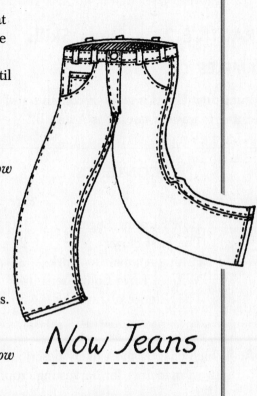

> You're a smart shopper. You know that great jeans are comfortable, good-looking, and made to last. You also know that great jeans cost too much. So, being a smart shopper, you wait until your favorite brand of jeans goes on sale. If you're lucky, you'll find a pair that's the exact size, style, and color you're looking for. But chances are, you won't.
>
> So, what's the smart shopper to do? Buy *Now Jeans! Now Jeans* are made of 100% preshrunk cotton denim in four colors. And we double-stitch our seams for extra strength and wear. *Now Jeans* come in 5 different styles and 30 sizes, so you will find a pair that really fits. Inch for inch, *Now Jeans* have the looks, quality, and comfort of those expensive brands. They just cost less!
>
> So stop waiting for sales. Go right to your favorite department store and buy a pair of *Now Jeans.* That's what smart shoppers do.
>
> *Now Jeans*

10. Which idea from this ad is a fact?

Ⓐ You're a smart shopper.

Ⓑ Great jeans are good looking.

Ⓒ Great jeans cost too much.

Ⓓ *Now Jeans* come in four colors.

11. This advertisement tries to persuade you to buy *Now Jeans* instead of your favorite brand of jeans mainly by stating that *Now Jeans* are –

Ⓐ less expensive

Ⓑ more comfortable

Ⓒ better looking

Ⓓ more durable

12. Which idea from this advertisement is an opinion?

Ⓐ The seams of *Now Jeans* are double-stitched.

Ⓑ There are 5 styles and 30 sizes of *Now Jeans.*

Ⓒ Shoppers who are smart buy *Now Jeans.*

Ⓓ *Now Jeans* are sold in department stores.

Stop

Language Arts

PRACTICE 26 • Study Skills

SAMPLES

Directions: Use this table of contents and part of an index from a book on farming to answer questions A and B.

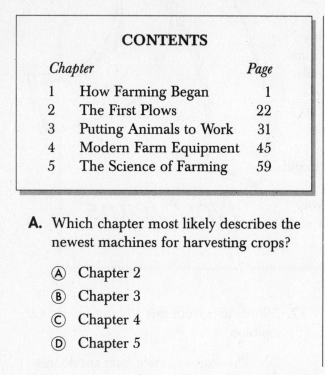

A. Which chapter most likely describes the newest machines for harvesting crops?

   Ⓐ Chapter 2

   Ⓑ Chapter 3

   Ⓒ Chapter 4

   Ⓓ Chapter 5

B. To find out how farmers keep diseases from spoiling their crops, you should read

   Ⓐ page 8

   Ⓑ page 20

   Ⓒ page 49

   Ⓓ page 62

Tips and Reminders

- Use key words in the question to figure out what information is needed.

- Study each part of a book or other visual aid carefully and use it to find the information you need.

- To find an index heading, look for a main topic that describes the others.

Go On

PRACTICE

Directions: Choose the best answer to each question about locating information.

1. Which set of guide words could be found on the dictionary page that includes the word *penny?*

    Ⓐ pearl/peddler

    Ⓑ peel/peg

    Ⓒ pebble/peculiar

    Ⓓ pelican/people

2. Which set of guide words could be found on the dictionary page that includes the word *famous?*

    Ⓐ fantastic/faraway

    Ⓑ faculty/failure

    Ⓒ false/fancy

    Ⓓ fashion/faulty

3. Which is a main index heading that includes the other three words?

    Ⓐ Landform

    Ⓑ Mountain

    Ⓒ Plateau

    Ⓓ Mesa

4. If you wanted to find information in an encyclopedia about Spanish explorers who met the Aztecs in Central America, you should look under

    Ⓐ Spanish

    Ⓑ explorers

    Ⓒ Aztec

    Ⓓ Central America

5. An encyclopedia would be the best reference source for finding

    Ⓐ an explanation of how a submarine works

    Ⓑ addresses of recycling centers in various states

    Ⓒ a list of local clubs and organizations

    Ⓓ the origin of the word *braid*

6. An atlas would be the best reference source for finding

    Ⓐ a map of Central America

    Ⓑ world records set by runners

    Ⓒ a description of how a fish breathes

    Ⓓ effective exercises for losing weight

7. Which type of information would you be most likely to find in a newspaper?

    Ⓐ a diagram of a lightbulb

    Ⓑ a list of products made from petroleum

    Ⓒ a summary of the President's latest speech

    Ⓓ a history of music around the world

8. A thesaurus would be the best reference source for finding which type of information?

    Ⓐ synonyms and antonyms of a word

    Ⓑ how to divide a word into syllables

    Ⓒ the language a word comes from

    Ⓓ how to pronounce a word

Go On →

Directions: Use this outline for a report about camping to answer questions 9–12.

I. Types of Camping Trips
  A. Forest
  B. Seashore
  C. Desert
  D. _____

II. Camping Gear
  A. Knives and axes
  B. Cooking utensils
  C. Backpacks
  D. Sleeping bags

III. _____
  A. Lean-to
  B. A-frame tent
  C. Dome tent

IV. Campfires
  A. Finding suitable firewood
  B. Types of campfires
  C. Building a fire in the rain

V. Health and Safety
  A. Avoiding dangerous animals
  B. Recognizing poisonous plants
  C. _____

9. Line I.D. in the outline is blank. Which of these best fits on line I.D.?

Ⓐ Planning
Ⓑ Camping supplies
Ⓒ Mountain
Ⓓ History of camping

10. Which of these would most likely be included in the part of the report based on section II of the outline?

Ⓐ Cook kits made of aluminum are lightweight and easy to pack.
Ⓑ Many state forests have areas set aside just for camping.
Ⓒ Evergreen branches can be used to make a lean-to.
Ⓓ Poison ivy has shiny green leaves that grow in groups of three.

11. Line III in the outline is blank. Which of these best fits on line III?

Ⓐ Choosing a camping site
Ⓑ Shelters
Ⓒ Planning meals
Ⓓ Emergencies

12. Which of these best fits on line V.C.?

Ⓐ Making water safe for drinking
Ⓑ How to choose gear
Ⓒ Goosedown sleeping bags
Ⓓ Backyard camping

Go On

Directions: Use this table of contents and part of an index from a book about dogs to answer questions 13–16.

CONTENTS

INDEX

13. On which page(s) should you look for information about how often you should wash a dog?

Ⓐ pages 74–75

Ⓑ page 77

Ⓒ page 79

Ⓓ pages 91–92

14. Which chapter is most likely to tell which dogs are best for someone who lives in an apartment?

Ⓐ Chapter 1   Ⓒ Chapter 4

Ⓑ Chapter 2   Ⓓ Chapter 6

15. To learn how much canned food a large dog should eat in a day, you should look on

Ⓐ page 7   Ⓒ page 46

Ⓑ page 31   Ⓓ page 51

16. Which of these is most likely to be found in Chapter 4?

Ⓐ a diagram that shows how to build a doghouse

Ⓑ a list of shots a dog should have

Ⓒ step-by-step directions for teaching a dog to sit

Ⓓ a photograph of a litter of puppies

Stop

Mathematics

PRACTICE 27 • Solving Problems

Directions: Choose the best answer to each problem.

SAMPLES

A. Park School students raised $235.00 at a car wash. They charged $5.00 per car. Which number sentence could be used to find out how many cars they washed?

   Ⓐ $235.00 \times \square = \$5.00$

   Ⓑ $235.00 \div \$5.00 = \square$

   Ⓒ $\square \div \$5.00 = \$235.00$

   Ⓓ $235.00 \times \$5.00 = \square$

B. Angie won a running race. She finished 43 seconds ahead of Eva, who came in second. What do you need to know to find how long it took Angie to complete the race?

   Ⓐ how many runners Eva beat

   Ⓑ what time the race started

   Ⓒ what distance the race covered

   Ⓓ how long Eva took to run the race

Tips and Reminders

- Underline or jot down important information to help you answer each question.

- Check each answer choice before choosing an answer.

- Draw a picture if it helps you answer the question.

- When a question asks <u>about</u> how many or how much, use rounding to estimate the answer.

PRACTICE

1. Mr. Lopez can type 47 words a minute on a computer. If he types for 30 minutes, <u>about</u> how many words will he type?

   Ⓐ 120

   Ⓑ 150

   Ⓒ 1200

   Ⓓ 1500

2. Lois was $60\frac{1}{4}$ inches tall last year. She is $62\frac{1}{2}$ inches tall this year. Which number sentence could be used to find out how much Lois grew in one year?

   Ⓐ $60\frac{1}{4} + \square = 62\frac{1}{2}$

   Ⓑ $62\frac{1}{2} + 60\frac{1}{4} = \square$

   Ⓒ $\square - 62\frac{1}{2} = 60\frac{1}{4}$

   Ⓓ $62\frac{1}{2} \div \square = 60\frac{1}{4}$

Go On

3. Mr. Jefferson paid $12.54 to fill his car with gasoline. The gasoline cost $1.39 per gallon. Which number sentence could be used to find out how many gallons of gasoline he bought?

Ⓐ $12.54 + $1.39 = □

Ⓑ $12.54 ÷ $1.39 = □

Ⓒ □ ÷ $1.39 = $12.54

Ⓓ $12.54 × □ = $1.39

4. Each section of the City Center's concert hall seats 350 people. There are 17 sections. Which number sentence could be used to find out how many people the concert hall seats?

Ⓐ 350 ÷ □ = 17

Ⓑ □ + 17 = 350

Ⓒ 350 × 17 = □

Ⓓ □ − 350 = 17

5. Sally wants to make 12 reprints of a photograph. Each reprint costs $2.79. <u>About</u> how much will she pay for the reprints?

Ⓐ $45.00   Ⓒ $15.00

Ⓑ $30.00   Ⓓ $9.00

6. Marta walked $8\frac{3}{4}$ miles. Her sister bicycled $5\frac{1}{2}$ times farther. <u>About</u> how far did Marta's sister bicycle?

Ⓐ 15 miles   Ⓒ 40 miles

Ⓑ 25 miles   Ⓓ 50 miles

7. Mack is bringing a bag filled with aluminum cans to the recycling center, which pays 3¢ for each can. What do you need to know to find out how much money Mack will get for his cans?

Ⓐ how many cans are in the bag

Ⓑ how large the bag is

Ⓒ how much the bag weighs

Ⓓ how much each can weighs

8. Hank made $5\frac{1}{2}$ quarts of lemonade for the class picnic. When the picnic was over, there were $2\frac{2}{3}$ quarts left. Which number sentence could be used to find out how much lemonade Hank's class drank?

Ⓐ $5\frac{1}{2} ÷ □ = 2\frac{2}{3}$

Ⓑ $□ − 2\frac{2}{3} = 5\frac{1}{2}$

Ⓒ $2\frac{2}{3} + 5\frac{1}{2} = □$

Ⓓ $5\frac{1}{2} − □ = 2\frac{2}{3}$

9. Vera is up and dressed by 7:00 A.M. She spends 15 minutes eating and 20 minutes exercising. Then she reads until it's time to catch the school bus. What information do you need to find how long Vera spends reading?

Ⓐ what time the school bus comes

Ⓑ how fast she reads

Ⓒ how long she took to get dressed

Ⓓ how many exercises she did

95

Go On

10. Mrs. Maretta wants to order 300 balloons, which come in packages of 12. Which number sentence could be used to find how many packages she needs to order?

Ⓐ $12 + \square = 300$

Ⓑ $300 \div 12 = \square$

Ⓒ $12 \times 300 = \square$

Ⓓ $\square \div 12 = 300$

11. Mr. Yetter had $80.00 in his wallet. Then he spent $47.32 for groceries and $3.50 for newspapers. Which number sentence could be used to find how much money he has left?

Ⓐ $\$80.00 - (\$47.32 + \$3.50) = \square$

Ⓑ $\$80.00 - (\$47.32 - \$3.50) = \square$

Ⓒ $\$3.50 + \$47.32 = \square - \$80.00$

Ⓓ $\$47.32 - \$3.50 = \square - \$80.00$

12. Leonard earns $5.40 an hour bagging groceries at the supermarket. Last Saturday Leonard worked 9 hours. Which question can you answer with this information?

Ⓐ How many bags did Leonard pack?

Ⓑ How much money did Leonard make on Saturday?

Ⓒ How many shoppers did Leonard help that day?

Ⓓ At what time did Leonard start work on Saturday?

13. Helena has 417 baseball cards. She gives away 23 and buys 10 new cards. Which number sentence could be used to find out how many cards Helena has now?

Ⓐ $417 - (23 + 10) = \square$

Ⓑ $23 + 10 = 417 - \square$

Ⓒ $(417 - 23) + 10 = \square$

Ⓓ $23 - 10 = \square + 417$

14. Workers loaded 981 tires into 5 freight cars. If they put about the same number of tires into each freight car, what is the <u>approximate</u> size of each load?

Ⓐ 50 tires   Ⓒ 200 tires

Ⓑ 100 tires   Ⓓ 500 tires

15. The Meckler children ate $\frac{5}{12}$ of a large pizza, and the parents ate $\frac{1}{3}$. Which number sentence could be used to find out how much pizza was left?

Ⓐ $1 - \left(\frac{5}{12} + \frac{1}{3}\right) = \square$

Ⓑ $\square + \frac{1}{3} = 1 + \frac{5}{12}$

Ⓒ $1 + \left(\frac{5}{12} - \frac{1}{3}\right) = \square$

Ⓓ $\square - \frac{1}{3} = 1 - \frac{5}{12}$

16. Poster Land is taking $\frac{1}{3}$ off the regular price of movie posters. What is the approximate sale price of a movie poster that usually sells for $17.59?

Ⓐ $10.50   Ⓒ $14.50

Ⓑ $12.00   Ⓓ $16.00

PRACTICE 28 • Making Judgments

SAMPLES

Directions: Read this passage about health. Then answer questions A and B.

What are you supposed to do when you cough around other people? Cover your mouth, right? Actually, this action may be polite, but it is not healthful because it ensures that your hand gets covered with cold germs. You then spread these germs to everything you touch. Anyone who touches objects you have handled can pick up your germs and catch your cold.

So how should you keep your cold from spreading? You could wash your hands each time you cover a cough, but you may find yourself in situations where there is no sink nearby. A simpler solution is to cover your coughs with your elbow. This blocks germs just like covering coughs with your hand does. But since you don't handle objects with your elbows, you're less likely to spread your germs.

A. Which statement best expresses the author's beliefs about colds?

Ⓐ It's almost impossible to avoid getting a cold.

Ⓑ If you have a cold, try not to spread your germs.

Ⓒ Even the healthiest people get colds from time to time.

Ⓓ Colds are not serious, but they can lead to other illnesses.

B. The author's main purpose in this passage is to –

Ⓐ persuade readers to stay healthy

Ⓑ compare colds with fevers

Ⓒ give information about cold germs

Ⓓ describe what having a cold is like

Tips and Reminders

• To decide on the author's purpose or point of view, think about what the author is trying to say or why the author wrote the passage.

• To make a judgment or decision, think about the information in the passage. Look at all the answer choices and choose the most likely or most important one.

Go On

PRACTICE

Directions: Read this movie review. Then answer questions 1–4.

Four new movies open this week at Main Street Cinemas. Two are sure to be hits.

Scream Dream is director Lee Malone's new horror movie. *Scream Dream* tries to make your blood run cold, but it won't even give you a shiver. The plot has no surprises, the acting is terrible, and the special effects fall flat. Don't waste your money on this one.

Hollywood's biggest star, Mike Moore, can't shine brightly enough to make *Over the Edge* a success. Moore's character, a private detective, is just too heartless for the audience to like. The movie also jumps quickly from scene to scene in an attempt to build suspense. But this jumpiness leaves out so many details that the story is hard to follow.

Jack and the Beanstalk is a cartoon version of the famous fairy tale. The characters are beautifully drawn, and the music is wonderful. Young children may be wiggling restlessly at the end of this two-hour movie, but adults will enjoy every minute.

If you're looking for big laughs, *On the Road* is a movie you should not miss. As a pair of daffy scientists trying to travel through time, Jake Reese and Don Bruno have never been funnier together.

1. The author's main purpose in this passage is to –

   Ⓐ compare different movie actors

   Ⓑ give opinions about four movies

   Ⓒ explain how movies are made

   Ⓓ describe the local movie theater

2. Which statement best expresses how the author feels about *Scream Dream?*

   Ⓐ Lee Malone is the director.

   Ⓑ *Scream Dream* is a horror movie.

   Ⓒ *Scream Dream* tries to make your blood run cold.

   Ⓓ Don't waste your money on this one.

3. What is the main problem with the movie *Jack and the Beanstalk?*

   Ⓐ It has too much music.

   Ⓑ Its cartoons are not drawn well.

   Ⓒ It is too long for young children.

   Ⓓ It is a fairy tale.

4. According to the author, which of the four movies is most confusing?

   Ⓐ *Scream Dream*

   Ⓑ *Over the Edge*

   Ⓒ *Jack and the Beanstalk*

   Ⓓ *On the Road*

Go On →

PRACTICE 28 • Making Judgments (continued)

Directions: Read this passage about taxis in New York City. Then answer questions 5–8.

Catch a taxi in New York City and you just may find yourself riding in the car of the future. A large American car company is testing out new cars that run on natural gas. New York City taxis were chosen as the test cars. Why? New York City taxis run up lots of miles in the worst kind of stop-and-go traffic. If cars fueled by natural gas perform well in New York, they will be a success anywhere. Testing in New York also gives the company free advertising as it shows off its cars to the huge number of visitors who hail taxis there every day.

New York City's taxi drivers and residents also benefit from the test taxis. Natural gas is cheaper than gasoline, so drivers save money with every mile they drive. Natural gas is also a cleaner fuel than gasoline. Nearly half the city's air pollution is blamed on gasoline-fueled taxis. With large numbers of test taxis running on natural gas, the pollution is sure to decrease.

One problem taxi drivers must face is finding a place to fill up. Only a few stations in New York City sell natural gas. But more and more drivers are willing to deal with the problem and drive the test cars. For them, the future has come.

5. The author's main purpose in this passage is to –

  Ⓐ describe the new taxis being driven in New York City

  Ⓑ complain about pollution in New York City

  Ⓒ persuade service stations to supply natural gas for taxis

  Ⓓ explain why there are so many taxis in New York City

6. What is the author's attitude toward the taxis that use natural gas?

  Ⓐ amused

  Ⓑ approving

  Ⓒ suspicious

  Ⓓ worried

7. For residents of New York City, the best thing about the new taxis being tested there is that they –

  Ⓐ provide free advertising

  Ⓑ save money for taxi drivers

  Ⓒ may be used by visitors

  Ⓓ produce less air pollution

8. Which judgment is supported by information in the passage?

  Ⓐ New York has excellent taxi drivers.

  Ⓑ Driving in New York is hard on a car.

  Ⓒ Cars are the biggest source of pollution in the country.

  Ⓓ Taxis fueled by natural gas are sure to catch on quickly.

Go On

Directions: Read this passage about a man named Mathew Brady. Then answer questions 9–12.

In 1860, Mathew Brady was a famous photographer. He had built his reputation by taking pictures of presidents, writers, artists, and show business people. Brady's success made it possible for him to open a dazzling studio in New York. Rich people traveled there from all over the world to be photographed by Brady. As he snapped their pictures in the comfort and luxury of his studio, Brady did not know how his life was about to change.

Then the Civil War broke out in the United States. Brady understood the importance of the war and decided he should photograph it. With a team of 20 assistants, Brady took more than 3500 pictures of soldiers in battles and in camps during the four years of the Civil War. Brady's pictures made him even more famous. They also became a priceless record of one of our country's most trying times.

But Brady paid a huge price for the project. During the war, he spent more than $100,000 to buy supplies and pay his assistants. At the same time, he let his studio business slow down. Before long, Brady had many large debts. Brady never overcame his money problems. He died a poor man, and few remembered his earlier fame.

9. According to the passage, Brady's most important accomplishment was taking pictures of –

   (A) writers
   (B) artists
   (C) show business people
   (D) Civil War soldiers

10. Brady had the most trouble doing which of these things?

    (A) attracting customers
    (B) understanding the Civil War
    (C) managing his money
    (D) training his assistants

11. Which sentence best expresses the author's point of view toward Brady?

    (A) He wasted his life and his talent.
    (B) He made an important contribution to history.
    (C) He let people take advantage of him.
    (D) He was the best photographer who ever lived.

12. The author wrote this passage mainly to –

    (A) encourage people to take up photography as a hobby
    (B) explain how Brady's cameras worked
    (C) describe the achievements of Mathew Brady
    (D) help others avoid the mistakes Brady made

Stop

Language Arts

PRACTICE 29 • Reference Materials

SAMPLES

Directions: Use this part of a dictionary page to answer questions A, B, and C.

---

guess | gum

guile (gīl) *n.* Slyness; cleverness.

guilt•y (gĭl' tē) *adj.* **1.** Responsible for doing wrong or committing a crime. **2.** Filled with sorrowful knowledge of having done wrong.

gui•ro (gwîr' ō) *n.,* *pl.* **gui•ros.** A musical instrument from Latin America, made of a gourd with a rough surface, which is scraped with a stick to make sounds.

gul•li•ble (gul' ə bəl) *adj.* Easily fooled or tricked.

A. In which sentence is the second meaning of *guilty* used correctly?

Ⓐ You will *guilty* yourself if you have a sense of right and wrong.

Ⓑ The man was found *guilty* of stealing, so he must go to jail.

Ⓒ Joe felt so *guilty* about lying that he finally admitted the truth.

Ⓓ The students should *guilty* if they copied their reports from books.

B. What is a *guiro?*

Ⓐ a musical instrument

Ⓑ a quality of slyness

Ⓒ a place in Latin America

Ⓓ a long stick

C. Which entry word could also appear on this dictionary page?

Ⓐ guardian Ⓒ guppy

Ⓑ guffaw Ⓓ gusher

Tips and Reminders

• Look for key words to help answer each question.

• Study the excerpt, chart, or map carefully and use it to find the information you need.

• In a dictionary, guide words show the first and last entries on a dictionary page.

Go On →

PRACTICE

Directions: Use this part of a dictionary page to answer questions 1–5.

---

majesty | manner

ma•lev•o•lent (mə lev' ə lənt) *adj.* Wishing suffering or harm to others; spiteful.

mal•lard (mal' ərd) *n.* A common wild duck.

mam•bo (mäm' bō) *n., pl.* **mam•bos.** **1.** A Latin American dance similar to the rumba. **2.** Music for this type of dance. – *v.* To dance the mambo.

man•age (man' ij) *v.* **1.** To have or gain control over: *You must manage your temper.* **2.** To drive, operate, or run: *manage the electric drill.* **3.** To succeed in doing something: *We managed to finish our homework.* **4.** To direct or supervise: *manage the workers.*

man•do•lin (man' dəl in) *n.* A stringed instrument with a pear-shaped body.

Pronunciation Guide

a	pat	o	pot	ə represents
ā	pay	ō	go	*a* in *ago*
ä	father	ô	for	*e* in it*e*m
e	pet	ŏŏ	book	*i* in penc*i*l
ē	be	ōō	boot	*o* in at*o*m
i	pit	u	cut	*u* in circ*u*s
ī	pie	û	fur	

---

1. Which entry word could also appear on this dictionary page?

    Ⓐ manatee   Ⓒ mantle

    Ⓑ mansion   Ⓓ manufacture

2. The *a* in *mambo* is pronounced like the *a* in –

    Ⓐ pat   Ⓒ ago

    Ⓑ pay   Ⓓ father

3. What is a *mandolin?*

    Ⓐ a stringed instrument

    Ⓑ a Latin American dance

    Ⓒ a wild duck

    Ⓓ a kind of fruit

4. How many syllables are in *malevolent?*

    Ⓐ 3   Ⓒ 5

    Ⓑ 4   Ⓓ 6

5. Which definition of *manage* is used in this sentence?

    Did you *manage* to fix that old clock?

    Ⓐ v. 1   Ⓒ v. 3

    Ⓑ v. 2   Ⓓ v. 4

PRACTICE 29 • Reference Materials (continued)

Directions: Use this library catalog card to answer questions 6–8.

> **Leichester, Agnes**
> 592.7   Why they do that: animal
> **L41**   behaviors explained / by Agnes
>   Leichester; illustrated by Tobias
>   Gomez. Chicago: Fuller Jones, 1994
>   258 p.: ill.; 29 cm.
>
>   1. Animals 2. Behavior 3. Mammals
>   4. Reptiles I. Gomez, Tobias. II. Title

6. What is the title of this book?

- Ⓐ Leichester, Agnes
- Ⓑ Animal Behaviors Explained
- Ⓒ Mammals and Reptiles
- Ⓓ Why They Do That: Animal Behaviors Explained

7. Tobias Gomez is the name of the book's –

- Ⓐ author
- Ⓑ publisher
- Ⓒ illustrator
- Ⓓ narrator

8. Which number should you use to find this book in the library?

- Ⓐ 1994
- Ⓑ 592.7
- Ⓒ 258 p.
- Ⓓ 29 cm

Directions: Choose the best answer to each question about using an online library catalog system.

9. Ray Bradbury wrote several science fiction novels. To find the titles of the novels he wrote, you should look in the –

- Ⓐ AUTHOR file under "Bradbury"
- Ⓑ SUBJECT file under "Science"
- Ⓒ KEY WORD file under "Bradbury"
- Ⓓ SUBJECT file under "Novels"

10. If you want to find the call number for the book *To a Young Dancer*, you should begin by selecting which menu item?

- Ⓐ AUTHOR
- Ⓑ SUBJECT
- Ⓒ TITLE
- Ⓓ KEY WORD

11. Thurgood Marshall was the first African American to serve on the U.S. Supreme Court. To find a biography about him, you should search under –

- Ⓐ AUTHOR
- Ⓑ SUBJECT
- Ⓒ TITLE
- Ⓓ KEY WORD

12. If you wanted a list of every book in the library with the word "modern" in the title, which menu item should you select?

- Ⓐ AUTHOR
- Ⓑ SUBJECT
- Ⓒ TITLE
- Ⓓ KEY WORD

Go On

Directions: This map shows a country with five states. Use the map to answer 13–15.

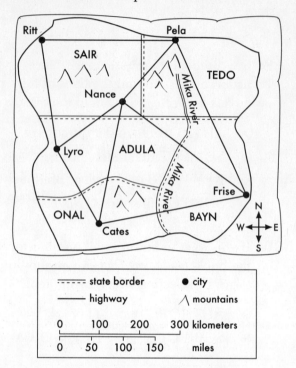

    ----- state border   ● city
    ——— highway   ∧ mountains

    0   100   200   300 kilometers
    |——————————————————————|
    0   50   100   150   miles

13. The Mika River flows through every state EXCEPT:

  Ⓐ Onal   Ⓒ Adula

  Ⓑ Sair   Ⓓ Bayn

14. In which direction would you travel from Frise to Pela?

  Ⓐ northwest   Ⓒ southwest

  Ⓑ northeast   Ⓓ southeast

15. About how many kilometers is the drive from Lyro to Nance?

  Ⓐ 50   Ⓒ 200

  Ⓑ 100   Ⓓ 400

Directions: This chart compares five telephone models. Use the chart to answer 16–18.

Telephones				
Model	Price	Type	Built-in Answering Machine	Ring volume(s)
CD-39	$$	🕻	no	L, M, S
LB-45	$$$	▯	yes	L, S
M-4	$$$	🕻	yes	L, M, S
TQ-17	$	▯	no	M
X-80	$$	▱	no	L, S

Key $ = $0–$30   🕻 = desk   L = loud

       $$ = $30–$50   ▯ = wall   M = medium

       $$$ = over $50   ▱ = cordless   S = soft

16. Which model might cost as much as $70.00?

  Ⓐ CD-39   Ⓒ TQ-17

  Ⓑ LB-45   Ⓓ X-80

17. Which model can be carried from room to room?

  Ⓐ LB-45   Ⓒ TQ-17

  Ⓑ M-4   Ⓓ X-80

18. Which statement best describes the M-4?

  Ⓐ It has only one ring volume.

  Ⓑ It costs less than $50.00.

  Ⓒ It has an answering machine.

  Ⓓ It is a cordless phone.

Mathematics

PRACTICE 30 • Word Problems

Directions: Solve each problem.

SAMPLES

A. Tricia bought three notebooks for $5.50, $2.79, and $1.95. What was the total cost of the notebooks?

  Ⓐ $9.24   Ⓒ $10.24

  Ⓑ $10.14   Ⓓ $11.24

B. Mr. Spencer drove his truck 261 miles on Thursday, 321 miles on Friday, and 276 miles on Saturday. What is the average number of miles he drove per day?

  Ⓐ 179 miles   Ⓒ 276 miles

  Ⓑ 189 miles   Ⓓ 286 miles

Tips and Reminders

- Figure out what you have to do in each problem and write a number sentence to help you find the answer.

- Draw a picture or make a table if it will help you solve the problem.

- If you have trouble solving the problem, try each answer choice to see which one works.

PRACTICE

1. Sam bought a bottle of shampoo and a tube of toothpaste. He paid for them with a $20.00 bill.

How much change should Sam receive?

  Ⓐ $1.88   Ⓒ $11.88

  Ⓑ $8.12   Ⓓ $12.88

2. Justin starts walking to school at 7:40. School starts at 8:15.

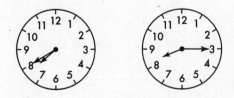

If it takes Justin 25 minutes to walk to school, how many minutes early will he arrive?

  Ⓐ 5 min   Ⓒ 15 min

  Ⓑ 10 min   Ⓓ 25 min

Go On

3. Tess put a pie in the oven at 4:35. It must bake for 55 minutes. Then it must cool for 30 minutes. At what time can Tess serve the pie?

Ⓐ 5:00   Ⓒ 5:30

Ⓑ 5:05   Ⓓ 6:00

4. Debbie and Juan rowed $\frac{1}{4}$ mile from the beach to the island. Then they rowed $\frac{5}{6}$ mile to the dock. How far did they row altogether?

Ⓐ $\frac{3}{12}$ mile   Ⓒ $\frac{10}{12}$ mile

Ⓑ $\frac{7}{12}$ mile   Ⓓ $1\frac{1}{12}$ miles

5. There are four children in the MacGregor family. Scott is shorter than Bonnie. Vera is taller than Elaine. Bonnie is shorter than Elaine. Who is the tallest child?

Ⓐ Bonnie   Ⓒ Elaine

Ⓑ Vera   Ⓓ Scott

6. Tina has 96 pictures in her photo album, and $\frac{3}{16}$ of them are pictures of her dog. How many of the pictures are of Tina's dog?

Ⓐ 16   Ⓒ 32

Ⓑ 18   Ⓓ 48

7. Theo has 4 sweatshirts and 3 pairs of sweatpants. How many different outfits of one sweatshirt and one pair of sweatpants can he make?

Ⓐ 7   Ⓒ 15

Ⓑ 12   Ⓓ 24

8. On Monday Seth practiced his tuba for 25 minutes. He practiced 40 minutes on Tuesday, 20 minutes on Wednesday, and 55 minutes on Friday. What is the average time Seth spent practicing each day?

Ⓐ 25 min   Ⓒ 35 min

Ⓑ 28 min   Ⓓ 40 min

9. A paper bag holds 8 red crayons, 4 blue crayons, 2 yellow crayons, and 6 green crayons. If you take one crayon from the bag without looking, what is the probability of drawing a red crayon?

Ⓐ $\frac{3}{5}$ Ⓒ $\frac{1}{12}$

Ⓑ $\frac{2}{5}$ Ⓓ $\frac{1}{20}$

10. If 6 new tires for the school bus cost a total of $693.00, how much did each tire cost?

Ⓐ $11.50   Ⓒ $115.00

Ⓑ $11.55   Ⓓ $115.50

Go On

11. It took 135 bags of gravel to cover the playground. One bag weighs 25.75 pounds. How many pounds of gravel were needed to cover the playground?

Ⓐ 260.75 lb   Ⓒ 3476.25 lb
Ⓑ 315.5 lb   Ⓓ 3925 lb

12. Mr. Beal, Ms. Green, and Mrs. Hart work at the bank. Mr. Beal works Monday, Tuesday, and Wednesday. Ms. Green works Tuesday, Thursday, and Saturday. Mrs. Hart works Wednesday, Thursday, and Friday. What day is it if Mr. Beal and Ms. Green are both working and Mrs. Hart has the day off?

Ⓐ Tuesday   Ⓒ Thursday
Ⓑ Wednesday   Ⓓ Friday

13. Stacey uses 7 yards of fabric to make a twin-size bedspread and 10 yards of fabric for a full-size bedspread. At this rate, how much fabric will she need for 3 twin-size and 2 full-size bedspreads?

Ⓐ 22 yd   Ⓒ 41 yd
Ⓑ 35 yd   Ⓓ 50 yd

14. A number cube is numbered 1–6. If you toss the cube once, what is the probability of rolling an even number?

Ⓐ $\frac{1}{6}$ Ⓒ $\frac{1}{2}$
Ⓑ $\frac{1}{3}$ Ⓓ $\frac{2}{3}$

The table below shows the length of different trails. Use the table to answer 15–16.

Trail	Length (miles)
Lookout Trail	$2\frac{3}{4}$
Summit Trail	$4\frac{1}{4}$
Sterling Lake	$\frac{7}{8}$
Ridge Trail	$3\frac{1}{2}$

15. How much longer is the Summit Trail than the Ridge Trail?

Ⓐ $\frac{1}{2}$ mile   Ⓒ $1\frac{1}{4}$ miles
Ⓑ $\frac{3}{4}$ mile   Ⓓ $1\frac{1}{2}$ miles

16. If Jeff hikes the Lookout Trail and Amy hikes to Sterling Lake, how many miles will Jeff and Amy walk in all?

Ⓐ $1\frac{7}{8}$ miles   Ⓒ $2\frac{5}{8}$ miles
Ⓑ $2\frac{3}{4}$ miles   Ⓓ $3\frac{5}{8}$ miles

17. Hal bought turkey, lettuce, and cheese for sandwiches. How many different kinds of sandwiches can he make by combining any two of these foods?

Ⓐ 6   Ⓒ 3
Ⓑ 4   Ⓓ 2

18. Mike earned $23.91 in April, $30.36 in May, and $27.75 in June. What is the average amount he earned per month?

Ⓐ $82.02   Ⓒ $27.34
Ⓑ $41.01   Ⓓ $20.50

Go On →

19. Mr. Rozak bought 12 packages of tulip bulbs for his garden and his mother's garden. Each package contains 8 bulbs. If Mr. Rozak plants 59 bulbs, how many will be left for his mother's garden?

Ⓐ 20   ⓒ 47
Ⓑ 37   Ⓓ 71

20. One roll of Magic Towels costs $1.59. A package of 3 rolls costs $3.99.

How much can be saved on 3 rolls by buying the package?

Ⓐ $0.26   ⓒ $1.33
Ⓑ $0.78   Ⓓ $2.40

21. Madison Middle School has 434 students. Of those students, $\frac{2}{7}$ are sixth-graders. How many are sixth-graders?

Ⓐ 31   ⓒ 124
Ⓑ 62   Ⓓ 407

22. At 5:00 A.M. the temperature was ⁻5°F. If the temperature rose 15 degrees by 12:00 noon, what was the temperature at noon?

Ⓐ ⁻20°F   ⓒ 15°F
Ⓑ 10°F   Ⓓ 20°F

23. Liza has 5 library books that are 6 days overdue. She has 3 other books that are 4 days overdue. The overdue fine at the library is $0.03 a day for each book.

6 DAYS   4 DAYS

What fine must Liza pay if she returns all her books today?

Ⓐ $0.18   ⓒ $1.26
Ⓑ $0.42   Ⓓ $3.60

24. A machine produced 800 nails in 4 minutes. At this rate, how long would it take the machine to produce 24,000 nails?

Ⓐ 1 hr 20 min   ⓒ 1 hr 40 min
Ⓑ 1 hr 30 min   Ⓓ 2 hr

25. A company packs 11 computer disks in a box. About how many disks are there in 790 boxes?

Ⓐ 8500   ⓒ 7500
Ⓑ 8000   Ⓓ 7000

26. Miguel earns $35,590 per year. About how much does he earn per month?

Ⓐ $2000   ⓒ $4000
Ⓑ $3000   Ⓓ $5000

Post-test

READING: Vocabulary

Directions: Find the word that means the same, or almost the same, as the underlined word.

1. with <u>zest</u>

    Ⓐ honesty   Ⓒ time

    Ⓑ help   Ⓓ enjoyment

2. street <u>vendor</u>

    Ⓐ sign   Ⓒ corner

    Ⓑ seller   Ⓓ curb

3. a <u>radiant</u> smile

    Ⓐ shining   Ⓒ regretful

    Ⓑ weak   Ⓓ quick

4. <u>lease</u> a building

    Ⓐ sell   Ⓒ rent

    Ⓑ vacate   Ⓓ buy

5. to <u>fortify</u>

    Ⓐ enlist   Ⓒ enter

    Ⓑ follow   Ⓓ strengthen

6. <u>artificial</u> fruit

    Ⓐ fake   Ⓒ ripe

    Ⓑ tasty   Ⓓ juicy

Directions: Find the word that means the OPPOSITE of the underlined word.

7. in her <u>absence</u>

    Ⓐ shadow   Ⓒ presence

    Ⓑ loss   Ⓓ attitude

8. a <u>merciful</u> man

    Ⓐ kind   Ⓒ hopeful

    Ⓑ cruel   Ⓓ proud

Directions: Read the two sentences. Find the word that best fits the meaning of **both** sentences.

9. The eggs will _____ tomorrow.

Two seamen opened the _____.

    Ⓐ break   Ⓒ ship

    Ⓑ window   Ⓓ hatch

10. Tilly served lunch at the _____.

This law runs _____ to our interests.

    Ⓐ shelf   Ⓒ counter

    Ⓑ table   Ⓓ along

11. The water-skier followed in the _____ of the boat.

Please don't _____ the baby.

    Ⓐ wake   Ⓒ tease

    Ⓑ stream   Ⓓ feed

Go On

READING: Vocabulary (continued)

Directions: Read the sentences. Choose the word that best completes the meaning of each sentence.

Eight field hockey teams from different parts of the state entered the __(12)__. The Hornets were favored to win, but they were __(13)__ in the first game by the Seahorses. After winning three more games, the Seahorses emerged __(14)__ and became state champs.

12. (A) arena
    (B) tournament
    (C) schedule
    (D) party

13. (A) pleased
    (B) ignored
    (C) invited
    (D) defeated

14. (A) victorious
    (B) playful
    (C) upset
    (D) worthy

Directions: Choose the meaning of the underlined prefix or suffix.

15. <u>auto</u>biography   <u>auto</u>graph
    (A) before   (C) self
    (B) against   (D) without

16. <u>il</u>legal   <u>il</u>logical
    (A) not   (C) across
    (B) beyond   (D) with

17. life<u>like</u>   child<u>like</u>
    (A) without
    (B) in the direction of
    (C) one who
    (D) relating to

18. enlarge<u>ment</u>   amuse<u>ment</u>
    (A) lacking
    (B) state or quality of
    (C) belonging to
    (D) less of

Directions: Read the sentence and the question. Find the word that best answers the question.

19. Mari was _____ to enter the room.
    Which word suggests that she was unsure?
    (A) anxious
    (B) proud
    (C) excited
    (D) reluctant

20. Ken looked at me with a _____ grin.
    Which word suggests that Ken is greedy?
    (A) kindly
    (B) selfish
    (C) welcoming
    (D) silly

21. Plants will _____ in the greenhouse.
    Which word suggests that the plants will do well?
    (A) thrive
    (B) grow
    (C) wilt
    (D) stay

Stop

Post-test

READING: Comprehension

Directions: Read each passage. Choose the best answer to each question.

What are we doing to save the animals?

For several decades, people have worked to protect and preserve endangered species. Sometimes these changes take the world by storm; sometimes they occur in small steps.

In the 1970s and 1980s, many Americans became aware that dolphins were being trapped in nets used to catch tuna. Many people took part in wide-scale protests and boycotts of canned tuna products. As a result, the fishing industry developed new nets that kept dolphins safe. These new nets are better for everyone.

On a smaller scale, one couple has decided to try to save Australia's kangaroos. As the result of development, humans and kangaroos increasingly inhabit the same territories. Adult kangaroos are often injured as they jump across highways. One Australian family adopts baby kangaroos, or joeys, whose mothers have been injured or killed in auto accidents. They feed the joeys from a bottle and teach them to eat solid foods as they grow. The kangaroos' favorite is any food flavored with garlic. When the kangaroos are ready, the family releases them into the wilderness.

---

22. Which statement is an opinion?

Ⓐ Adult kangaroos are often injured.

Ⓑ Dolphins were being trapped in nets.

Ⓒ The new nets are better for everyone.

Ⓓ One Australian family adopts joeys.

23. Which title best states the main idea of this passage?

Ⓐ "Saving Endangered Species"

Ⓑ "One Step at a Time"

Ⓒ "Adopting Joeys"

Ⓓ "Anything with Garlic"

24. The changes "take the world by storm" means that they –

Ⓐ cause lightning and thunder

Ⓑ come about dramatically

Ⓒ involve many small steps

Ⓓ cause injuries and damage

25. According to this passage, what is the most serious threat to both dolphins and kangaroos?

Ⓐ lack of food

Ⓑ dangerous nets

Ⓒ human activities

Ⓓ automobile accidents

Go On →

What is Rosh Hashanah?

The Jewish New Year, Rosh Hashanah, is unlike New Year's Day in most Western countries. It takes place in the fall, in September or October, rather than on January 1. The year traditionally begins with the blowing of the *shofar*, which is a curved ram's horn. The *shofar* makes a sound similar to the noisemakers blown by other New Year's revelers.

There are several special foods associated with the holiday as well. After lighting candles and saying prayers over egg bread called *challah*, people then dip apple slices into honey. This symbolizes hopes for a sweet new year. A traditional meal might include homemade chicken soup with *kreplach*, which is chopped meat in a noodle wrapper, much like Chinese wonton. Then diners might eat a noodle or potato pudding and chicken or sliced beef. Finally, dessert usually includes cakes or other sweets made with honey.

---

26. The passage says, "This <u>symbolizes</u> hopes for a sweet new year." <u>Symbolizes</u> means –

   Ⓐ encourages

   Ⓑ represents

   Ⓒ invites

   Ⓓ follows

27. The *shofar* is blown to –

   Ⓐ make everyone quiet down

   Ⓑ scare people away

   Ⓒ signal the end of the celebration

   Ⓓ welcome the new year

28. How is Rosh Hashanah different from New Year's Day in most Western countries?

   Ⓐ It occurs in the fall.

   Ⓑ People make noise.

   Ⓒ It takes place on January 1.

   Ⓓ People eat favorite foods.

29. In a traditional celebration, when do people eat chicken soup?

   Ⓐ after eating cake

   Ⓑ after saying prayers

   Ⓒ before lighting candles

   Ⓓ before blowing the *shofar*

Exploring the Ocean Floor

In the past, divers could search for the wrecks of old ships only in fairly shallow waters. But in the 1980s, scientists and photographers began developing new equipment that could go far deeper than any human diver to send back televised images.

In 1985, using such equipment, scientist Robert D. Ballard and photographer Emory Kristof located the wreck of the British luxury liner *Titanic* a full two miles below the surface of the North Atlantic. The following year they used a small robot submarine to capture dramatic photographs of the legendary ship, lost since 1912.

Today's submarine robots are much more advanced. They are built to withstand the harmful effects of salt water and the crushing pressures of the ocean. With their strong but precise computer-controlled "hands," they can pick up anything from a heavy ship's bell to a delicate piece of glassware.

Now many ships that have been lost for centuries are about to be found. Their discovery will help historians gain new knowledge of early shipbuilding, ancient trade routes, and much more. At the same time, the lure of gold may attract treasure hunters who will destroy priceless ancient vessels in their rush to carry off treasures. Despite this concern, those who study the oceans are excited about the new age of ocean-floor exploration that has just begun.

---

30. This passage implies that –

  (A) scientists no longer want to study undersea life

  (B) historians are wealthy

  (C) the *Titanic* could not be located before 1985

  (D) submarines cause pollution

31. Newly developed equipment will help historians mainly by enabling them to –

  (A) find gold and other treasures

  (B) take pictures

  (C) pick up objects

  (D) gain knowledge

32. The author of this passage seems to feel that technology is –

  (A) beneficial to scientists

  (B) wasteful

  (C) dangerous to everyone

  (D) harmful to the environment

33. Which phrase does the author use to imply that the ocean poses dangerous obstacles for explorers?

  (A) "computer-controlled"

  (B) "early shipbuilding"

  (C) "delicate piece of glassware"

  (D) "crushing pressures"

The Perfect Gift

"Let's stop at TeenTunes and look at the new CDs," Trina suggested.

"Hey, doesn't anybody care about clothes anymore?" Suleika complained. "What's wrong with this group?"

"What level are we on?" asked Jeff. "I think we should go to Level Three."

As the friends wandered past the shops and looked around for familiar faces, Masha smiled to herself. Serious shopping wasn't the point of this outing. Passing the time together was. Masha glanced casually into various shops, content just to be with her friends. Suddenly she stopped at a jeweler's window and stared at a pair of cufflinks—silver, with inlaid blue stones. At that moment she knew what to get for her father's birthday, which was only a month away.

The others moved on, but Masha was transfixed. The cufflinks were so perfect. They would be the nicest present she had ever given her father. She squinted to read the price tag—and her heart sank. It just wouldn't be possible.

Trina called from the foot of the escalator. "Hey, Mash, come on! We're going up a level to have lunch." As Masha turned from the window, a small sign caught her eye: "Help Wanted, Part Time."

"I'll catch up with you," she called. "There's something I have to do."

---

34. When does this story take place?

(A) at night

(B) in late afternoon

(C) around noontime

(D) early in the morning

35. Which word best describes Masha?

(A) self-conscious

(B) embarrassed

(C) playful

(D) determined

36. The author's main purpose in writing this passage is to –

(A) entertain

(B) teach a lesson

(C) describe jewelry

(D) give information

37. What is Masha's problem in this story?

(A) She doesn't like her friends.

(B) She cannot afford the cufflinks.

(C) She does not have any nice clothes.

(D) She feels ill.

38. The others in the group seem to be different from Masha because they are most concerned with –

(A) making new friends

(B) getting to know each other

(C) shopping

(D) making their own gifts

Stop

Post-test

LANGUAGE ARTS: Mechanics and Usage

Directions: Read each sentence and look at the underlined word or words. Look for a mistake in capitalization, punctuation, or word usage. If you find a mistake, choose the best way to write the underlined part of the sentence. If there is no mistake, fill in the bubble beside answer D, "Correct as is."

1. Terry <u>brang</u> her dog to school.

ⓐ bringed
ⓑ bringing
ⓒ brought
ⓓ Correct as is

2. Gary <u>has wrote</u> two letters, but he hasn't mailed them.

ⓐ has written
ⓑ is written
ⓒ has writed
ⓓ Correct as is

3. When a bluebird landed on the railing, Tom took a picture of <u>them</u>.

ⓐ they   ⓒ it
ⓑ this   ⓓ Correct as is

4. The party was <u>truly</u> delightful.

ⓐ true   ⓒ truest
ⓑ truer   ⓓ Correct as is

5. Neither Jim <u>nor</u> Effie returned my call.

ⓐ and   ⓒ but
ⓑ or   ⓓ Correct as is

6. Turkey is a <u>traditionaler</u> choice for Thanksgiving than ham or fish.

ⓐ more traditional
ⓑ traditionalest
ⓒ most traditional
ⓓ Correct as is

7. She <u>hadn't never</u> planned to go.

ⓐ had not never
ⓑ had never
ⓒ had ever
ⓓ Correct as is

8. We moved to <u>canada on May 1 1997</u>.

ⓐ Canada on May 1 1997
ⓑ canada on May 1, 1997
ⓒ Canada on May 1, 1997
ⓓ Correct as is

9. "<u>Jen,</u> please come inside," said Dad.

ⓐ "Jen'   ⓒ "Jen
ⓑ "Jen: ⓓ Correct as is

10. Leo named all three <u>capitals,</u> Dover, Annapolis, and Concord.

ⓐ capitals.   ⓒ capitals"
ⓑ capitals: ⓓ Correct as is

11. We read a poem called <u>"fire and ice."</u>

ⓐ "Fire and ice."   ⓒ "Fire and Ice."
ⓑ "Fire And Ice."   ⓓ Correct as is

Go On

LANGUAGE ARTS: Mechanics and Usage (continued)

Directions: Read the sentences. Find the underlined word that has a mistake in spelling. If there are no mistakes in spelling, fill in the bubble beside answer D, "No mistake."

12. Ⓐ Ally is quite <u>bashful</u>.
    Ⓑ She doesn't like to be <u>notised</u>.
    Ⓒ <u>Occasionally</u> I tease her about it.
    Ⓓ No mistake

13. Ⓐ A <u>policeman</u> watched us.
    Ⓑ He was looking for <u>criminals</u>.
    Ⓒ Of course, we were <u>inocent</u>.
    Ⓓ No mistake

14. Ⓐ The <u>senator</u> shook my hand.
    Ⓑ She will win the <u>election</u>.
    Ⓒ I gave her a <u>donation</u>.
    Ⓓ No mistake

15. Ⓐ Keanu <u>scrambled</u> for the ball.
    Ⓑ Joey <u>takled</u> him.
    Ⓒ Keanu was <u>injured</u>.
    Ⓓ No mistake

16. Ⓐ John <u>implied</u> that I was wrong.
    Ⓑ Ken <u>suggested</u> a new idea.
    Ⓒ We found a <u>solution</u>.
    Ⓓ No mistake

17. Ⓐ That car is a <u>beuty</u>.
    Ⓑ I have never <u>driven</u> it.
    Ⓒ It is very <u>comfortable</u>.
    Ⓓ No mistake

Directions: Find the answer that is a complete sentence written correctly.

18. Ⓐ Philip made a diorama.
    Ⓑ He used a shoebox he painted action figures.
    Ⓒ A battle in the Civil War.
    Ⓓ Interesting and true to life.

19. Ⓐ Backed up and hit the stop sign.
    Ⓑ Millie, being upset but unhurt.
    Ⓒ Millie stopped the car she shut it off.
    Ⓓ There was no damage.

20. Ⓐ Playing soccer in the muddy field.
    Ⓑ Pearl kicked the ball toward the net.
    Ⓒ The goalie missed Pearl scored.
    Ⓓ Won the game by one goal.

21. Ⓐ Everyone was impressed by Roger's giant jack-o'-lantern.
    Ⓑ With diamond-shaped eyes and jagged teeth.
    Ⓒ The prize for the best pumpkin.
    Ⓓ The wind blew the candle went out.

22. Ⓐ Farouk, climbing onto the train.
    Ⓑ It was a steam train the steam poured from the stack.
    Ⓒ Wearing his new hat.
    Ⓓ Later, Farouk realized that he had left his hat on the train.

LANGUAGE ARTS: Composition

Directions: Read each paragraph. Then answer the questions that follow.

Paragraph 1

They live on the island of Komodo in Indonesia. Komodo lies west of Australia. It is located south of Malaysia. People thought that Komodo dragons were mythological creatures until members of a Dutch expedition sighted some of them in 1912.

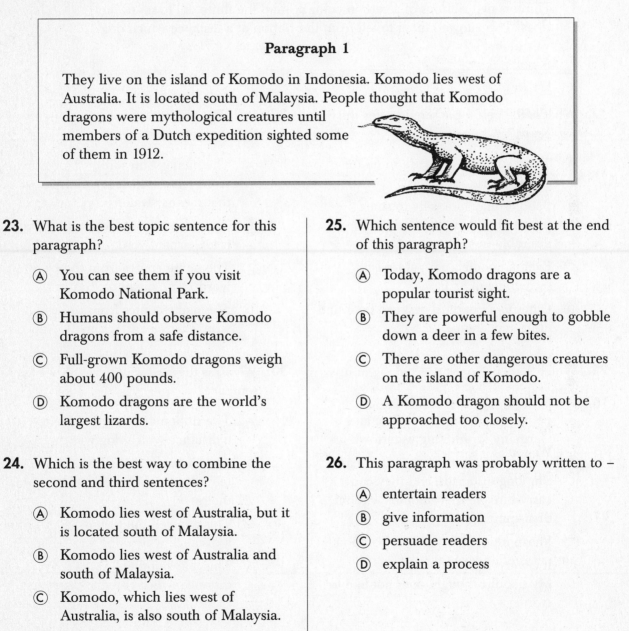

---

23. What is the best topic sentence for this paragraph?

  Ⓐ You can see them if you visit Komodo National Park.

  Ⓑ Humans should observe Komodo dragons from a safe distance.

  Ⓒ Full-grown Komodo dragons weigh about 400 pounds.

  Ⓓ Komodo dragons are the world's largest lizards.

24. Which is the best way to combine the second and third sentences?

  Ⓐ Komodo lies west of Australia, but it is located south of Malaysia.

  Ⓑ Komodo lies west of Australia and south of Malaysia.

  Ⓒ Komodo, which lies west of Australia, is also south of Malaysia.

  Ⓓ Komodo lies west of Australia, it is located south of Malaysia.

25. Which sentence would fit best at the end of this paragraph?

  Ⓐ Today, Komodo dragons are a popular tourist sight.

  Ⓑ They are powerful enough to gobble down a deer in a few bites.

  Ⓒ There are other dangerous creatures on the island of Komodo.

  Ⓓ A Komodo dragon should not be approached too closely.

26. This paragraph was probably written to –

  Ⓐ entertain readers

  Ⓑ give information

  Ⓒ persuade readers

  Ⓓ explain a process

Go On

Paragraph 2

The name comes from the German word *pudel*. This German word means "water." Poodles were bred in France and Germany for hunting waterfowl. They have great stamina, they can run long distances, and they can carry birds in their mouths without damaging them. When a poodle swims, its pompon tail is often visible. My poodle, though, does not like to swim. Hunters tied ribbons of a certain color around the fluffy tail to mark their dogs. This allowed them to tell from the ribbon at a distance which dog was theirs.

27. What is the best topic sentence for this paragraph?

Ⓐ Their large chests made room for strong hearts and lungs.

Ⓑ Poodles may look silly to some people, but they have many desirable traits.

Ⓒ Even a poodle's haircut reveals something of its past.

Ⓓ Clues to a poodle's past can be found in its appearance.

28. Which sentence does **not** belong in this paragraph?

Ⓐ Poodles were bred in France and Germany for hunting waterfowl.

Ⓑ They have great stamina, they can run long distances, and they can carry birds in their mouths without damaging them.

Ⓒ When a poodle swims, its pompon tail is often visible.

Ⓓ My poodle, though, does not like to swim.

29. Which is the best way to combine the first two sentences?

Ⓐ The name comes from the German word *pudel,* which is a German word that means "water."

Ⓑ The name comes from *pudel,* which is a German word.

Ⓒ The name comes from the German word *pudel,* meaning "water."

Ⓓ The name comes from a German word that means "water."

30. Which is the best way to revise the last sentence?

Ⓐ The ribbon allowed them to tell from a distance which dog was theirs.

Ⓑ At a distance, this allowed them to tell from the ribbon which dog was theirs.

Ⓒ This allowed the ribbon to tell from a distance which dog was theirs.

Ⓓ This allowed them to tell from a distance which ribbon was theirs.

Stop

LANGUAGE ARTS: Study Skills

Directions: Choose the best answer to each question about finding information.

31. To find a map showing the location of the Alps, you should look in –

Ⓐ a newspaper

Ⓑ an atlas

Ⓒ a dictionary

Ⓓ a thesaurus

32. To find a list of movies playing in your area, you should look in –

Ⓐ a newspaper

Ⓑ an encyclopedia

Ⓒ a thesaurus

Ⓓ an atlas

33. To find a book about Cyrus McCormick, inventor of the reaper, you should look in an online library catalog under –

Ⓐ reaper   Ⓒ Cyrus

Ⓑ inventor   Ⓓ McCormick

34. Which name would come first in alphabetical order?

Ⓐ Pietà   Ⓒ Piesporter

Ⓑ Piedmont   Ⓓ Pierce

35. Which of these is a main heading that includes the other topics?

Ⓐ Biology   Ⓒ Chemistry

Ⓑ Physics   Ⓓ Science

Use the dictionary entry to answer questions 36–38.

ter•ra•pin (ter' ə pin) *n.* Any of several edible turtles found in North America.

ter•raz•zo (tə rä' tsō) *n.* A mosaic flooring made of stone chips and cement.

ter•rene (te rēn') *adj.* **1.** Of the world or the earth. **2.** Earthy. –*n.* **1.** The earth. **2.** An area or region.

Pronunciation Guide

ä as in father	ō as in hope
e as in pet	ə represents
ē as in me	*a* in *ago*
i as in it	*e* in *item*

36. The *e* in *terrapin* is pronounced like the *e* in –

Ⓐ pet   Ⓒ item

Ⓑ me   Ⓓ father

37. How many syllables are there in *terrazzo?*

Ⓐ 2   Ⓒ 4

Ⓑ 3   Ⓓ 5

38. The word *terrene* refers to –

Ⓐ a kind of turtle

Ⓑ stone and cement

Ⓒ a kind of flooring

Ⓓ the earth

Stop

Post-test

MATHEMATICS: Concepts and Applications

Directions: Choose the best answer to each question.

1. $400,000 + 70,000 + 300 + 50 =$

    (A) 400,735   (C) 470,350

    (B) 407,350   (D) 470,035

2. Which is another way to express $6 \times 6 \times 6 \times 6$?

    (A) 4×6 (C) 4^6

    (B) $6 + 4$ (D) 6^4

3. What is the value of **5** in 75,182?

    (A) 5 ten thousands

    (B) 5 thousands

    (C) 5 hundreds

    (D) 5 tens

4. What is 9128 rounded to the nearest hundred?

    (A) 10,000   (C) 9100

    (B) 9200   (D) 9000

5. What fraction of this square is shaded?

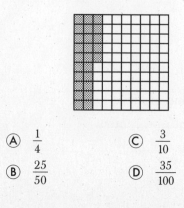

    (A) $\frac{1}{4}$ (C) $\frac{3}{10}$

    (B) $\frac{25}{50}$ (D) $\frac{35}{100}$

6. A number machine changes the number in the box at the top to the number in the box below it.

4	6	8	10
↓	↓	↓	↓
16	24	32	☐

What number goes in the empty box?

    (A) 20   (C) 40

    (B) 36   (D) 42

7. Which lists all the factors of 6?

    (A) 1, 6   (C) 2, 3, 6

    (B) 2, 3   (D) 1, 2, 3, 6

8. Which number sentence is true?

    (A) $^-20 < 20$

    (B) $^-20 > 0$

    (C) $^-20 > 20$

    (D) $^-20 = 20$

9. What is an equivalent fraction for $\frac{15}{18}$?

    (A) $\frac{3}{4}$ (C) $\frac{6}{7}$

    (B) $\frac{5}{6}$ (D) $\frac{5}{8}$

10. Which fraction is greatest?

    (A) $\frac{2}{3}$ (C) $\frac{3}{4}$

    (B) $\frac{5}{8}$ (D) $\frac{8}{9}$

Go On

11. Which decimal number has the same value as $\frac{4}{10}$?

Ⓐ 0.04

Ⓑ 0.4

Ⓒ 4.0

Ⓓ 0.410

12. Which number is greatest?

Ⓐ 0.36

Ⓑ 0.059

Ⓒ 0.008

Ⓓ 0.212

13. The 5 in 1.754 represents –

Ⓐ 5 thousandths

Ⓑ 5 hundredths

Ⓒ 5 tenths

Ⓓ 5 ones

14. What is 9.318 rounded to the nearest hundredth?

Ⓐ 9.319

Ⓑ 9.31

Ⓒ 9.3

Ⓓ 9.32

15. The arrow points to what number on the number line?

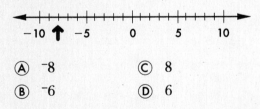

Ⓐ ⁻8   Ⓒ 8

Ⓑ ⁻6   Ⓓ 6

16. Which number goes in the circle to make this sentence true?

$(66 \times 14) \times \bigcirc = 66 \times (14 \times 32)$

Ⓐ 8   Ⓒ 32

Ⓑ 14   Ⓓ 66

17. Which point on the grid represents (1, 5)?

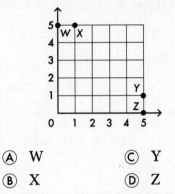

Ⓐ W   Ⓒ Y

Ⓑ X   Ⓓ Z

18. What is the diameter of a circle with a radius of 24 inches?

Ⓐ 12 in.   Ⓒ 48 in.

Ⓑ 36 in.   Ⓓ 72 in.

19. Which angle measures 180º?

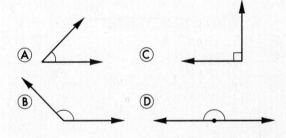

Go On

20. Which figure shows a rotation of 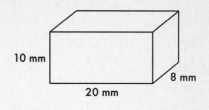 ?

Ⓐ

Ⓒ

Ⓑ

Ⓓ

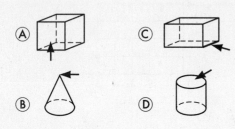

21. In which figure does the arrow point to an edge?

Ⓐ

Ⓒ

Ⓑ

Ⓓ

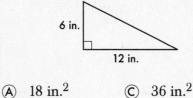

22. What is the perimeter of a rectangle that is 6 cm wide and 9.5 cm long?

Ⓐ 57 cm   Ⓒ 19 cm

Ⓑ 31 cm   Ⓓ 15.5 cm

23. What is the area of the triangle?

6 in.

12 in.

Ⓐ 18 in.^{2} Ⓒ 36 in.^{2}

Ⓑ 32 in.^{2} Ⓓ 72 in.^{2}

24. What is the volume of the rectangular prism?

10 mm

8 mm

20 mm

Ⓐ 160 mm^3 Ⓒ 800 mm^3

Ⓑ 320 mm^3 Ⓓ 1600 mm^3

25. Earl turned on the TV at 4:20. He turned it off at 5:15. How long was the TV on?

Ⓐ 45 min   Ⓒ 55 min

Ⓑ 50 min   Ⓓ 1 hour

26. What is the approximate distance from point A to point B? The scale is 1 cm = 10 m.

A ●————————————————● B

Ⓐ 50 m   Ⓒ 30 m

Ⓑ 40 m   Ⓓ 20 m

27. Gloria's driveway is 82 feet long. How many yards is that?

Ⓐ $16\frac{2}{3}$ yd   Ⓒ $27\frac{1}{3}$ yd

Ⓑ 21 yd   Ⓓ 41 yd

28. If $64 \div n = 16$, what is n?

Ⓐ 4   Ⓒ 12

Ⓑ 8   Ⓓ 16

MATHEMATICS: Concepts and Applications (continued)

Directions: Solve each problem. If the correct answer is Not Given, mark answer D, "NG."

29. The Garcias bought 78 gallons of heating oil at $1.04 per gallon. <u>About</u> how much did they pay for the oil?

    Ⓐ $70.00   Ⓒ $80.00

    Ⓑ $75.00   Ⓓ $85.00

30. Anne has 4 necklaces and 4 bracelets. How many different combinations of 1 necklace and 1 bracelet can she make?

    Ⓐ 8   Ⓒ 32

    Ⓑ 12   Ⓓ NG

Use the bar graph below to answer 31–32.

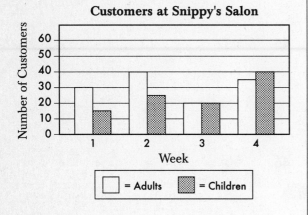

Customers at Snippy's Salon

☐ = Adults   ▓ = Children

31. In which week did Snippy's have the most customers?

    Ⓐ Week 1   Ⓒ Week 3

    Ⓑ Week 2   Ⓓ Week 4

32. In which week were there exactly twice as many adult customers as children?

    Ⓐ Week 1   Ⓒ Week 3

    Ⓑ Week 2   Ⓓ NG

33. There are 8 red blocks, 6 yellow blocks, 14 blue blocks, and 4 green blocks in a box. If you take out one block without looking, what is the probability that you will pick a yellow block?

    Ⓐ $\frac{1}{4}$

    Ⓑ $\frac{3}{16}$

    Ⓒ $\frac{3}{8}$

    Ⓓ NG

34. Mr. Collins's class wants to buy 32 copies of a book that costs $4.00. The class has collected $92.00. How much more money do they need?

    Ⓐ $28.00

    Ⓑ $36.00

    Ⓒ $128.00

    Ⓓ NG

35. At the Valley School, 3 out of 5 students are right-handed. If there are 200 students in the school, how many are left-handed?

    Ⓐ 100

    Ⓑ 150

    Ⓒ 180

    Ⓓ NG

36. Nick had $160.35 in his bank account. He baby-sat for 6 hours at $4.50 per hour and put his earnings in the bank account. Which number sentence should be used to find the total amount in his bank account?

    Ⓐ $160.35 + (6 × $4.50) = ☐

    Ⓑ 6 × ($160.35 + $4.50) = ☐

    Ⓒ $160.35 − (6 × $4.50) = ☐

    Ⓓ (6 × $4.50) − $160.35 = ☐

Stop

Post-test

MATHEMATICS: Computation

Directions: Find the answer to each problem. If the correct answer is not given, mark answer D, "None of these."

37. $9317 - 2248 =$

- (A) 7069
- (B) 7179
- (C) 11,565
- (D) None of these

38. $85 \times 100 =$

- (A) 850
- (B) 85,000
- (C) 850,000
- (D) None of these

39. $\begin{array}{r} 377 \\ \times\ 28 \\ \hline \end{array}$

- (A) 10,406
- (B) 10,456
- (C) 10,556
- (D) None of these

40. $6\overline{)505}$

- (A) 84
- (B) 84 R1
- (C) 85 R1
- (D) None of these

41. $2.88 + 4.79 =$

- (A) 6.67
- (B) 7.57
- (C) 7.77
- (D) None of these

42. $0.4 \times 0.9 =$

- (A) 3.6
- (B) 0.36
- (C) 0.036
- (D) None of these

43. $\begin{array}{r} 2\frac{5}{8} \\ + 1\frac{1}{8} \\ \hline \end{array}$

- (A) $3\frac{1}{2}$
- (B) $3\frac{5}{8}$
- (C) $3\frac{3}{4}$
- (D) None of these

44. $\begin{array}{r} \$355.09 \\ -\ 24.20 \\ \hline \end{array}$

- (A) \$330.89
- (B) \$331.29
- (C) \$379.29
- (D) None of these

45. $8\overline{)4.32}$

- (A) 0.054
- (B) 5.4
- (C) 54
- (D) None of these

46. $\frac{5}{6} + \frac{2}{3} =$

- (A) $\frac{7}{9}$
- (B) $1\frac{1}{2}$
- (C) $1\frac{1}{6}$
- (D) None of these

47. $\frac{1}{4} \times \frac{3}{5} =$

- (A) $\frac{1}{3}$
- (B) $\frac{4}{9}$
- (C) $\frac{3}{20}$
- (D) None of these

48. $\frac{3}{4} \div \frac{1}{8} =$

- (A) 6
- (B) $\frac{3}{32}$
- (C) $\frac{1}{6}$
- (D) None of these

Stop

Scoring Chart

Name _____ Class _____

Directions: Use this page to keep a record of your work. Make a check mark (✔) beside each test you finish. Then write your test score.

✔	PRETEST	Score	%
	Reading	/38	
	Language Arts	/38	
	Mathematics	/48	
	Total	/124	

✔	POST-TEST	Score	%
	Reading	/38	
	Language Arts	/38	
	Mathematics	/48	
	Total	/124	

✔	PRACTICE TEST	Score	%
	1. Synonyms/Antonyms	/28	
	2. Using Verbs	/14	
	3. Whole Number Concepts	/14	
	4. Context Clues	/18	
	5. Grammar and Usage	/8	
	6. Fractions/Decimals	/14	
	7. Word Analysis	/9	
	8. Sentences	/14	
	9. Number Operations	/12	
	10. Interpreting Text	/8	
	11. Punctuation	/10	
	12. Geometry	/16	
	13. Main Idea/Details	/10	
	14. Capitalization	/10	
	15. Measurement	/18	

✔	PRACTICE TEST	Score	%
	16. Text Structure	/10	
	17. Spelling	/15	
	18. Computation	/30	
	19. Inferences	/14	
	20. Combining Sentences	/10	
	21. Estimation	/12	
	22. Literary Elements	/11	
	23. Composition	/12	
	24. Interpreting Data	/16	
	25. Evaluating Information	/12	
	26. Study Skills	/16	
	27. Solving Problems	/16	
	28. Making Judgments	/12	
	29. Reference Materials	/18	
	30. Word Problems	/26	